# Conscious Business Development

# Conscious Business Development

How Business Owners and Leaders Can Become the
Engines That Create Value and Drive Wealth

Martin J. Harshberger

ISBN-13: 9780692051078
ISBN-10: 0692051074
Library of Congress Control Number: 2018930361
Measurable Results LLC, Saltillo, MS

# Contents

# About This book

The path to success is to take massive,
determined action.

—Tony Robbins

First, I wrote this book so that you could actually read it. I purposely kept it brief. The chapters are designed to give you information and examples for each step of the business-development process in a condensed format.

Second, I wrote this book to provide you, the business owner or CEO, a guide as well as a challenge on how to *consciously* succeed in business and in life.

The key word in the preceding statement is "consciously." I used "conscious" in the title to remind you that plan development and execution will take a *conscious* and concerted effort on your part. We all have hundreds of distractions in our life, and it's easy to rationalize excuses not to think strategically or not to focus on change or execution. Creating sustainable value in your business is not something you can delay indefinitely.

It's a huge statement for someone to say that a person can help you improve both your business and your life. But, for a lot of us, the two are closely aligned. Your business impacts your personal life in many ways. The stress, worry, and financial pressure caused by business issues can go home with you every night. I know I've been there. I founded and led a company that grew to require a million-dollar-per-month payroll. That represented a lot of families depending on my ability to keep the business sound.

I remember the struggles I had at the time. I learned from that experience that success in business or life requires *conscious* thinking, planning, and execution.

We've all been exposed to tools, technology, and processes promising great results and have had varying degrees of success in implementing what we've learned. We attend conferences or trade groups, hear excellent speakers, and become excited about trying the material in our organizations. And then, life happens, and no real change occurs. The initiative was doomed from the start because we didn't make a *conscious* effort to change our thinking.

The focus of this book is to help you change the way you think about your business and your life.

I've been truly blessed in my life. As I get older, I reflect on what I've accomplished and on how far I've come. I want to share that experience and help other business owners and CEOs travel the path to success a little more easily.

I certainly wasn't born to be a business expert. I was born and raised in Western Pennsylvania coal country in a small town of about three hundred people. I guess by today's standards we were poor. But since everyone else was too, it really wasn't obvious.

The lessons I learned growing up had nothing to do with business. My family members were coal miners and steelworkers, but they taught me all I needed to know about success.

Hard work is critical, but hard work alone isn't enough. The folks where I grew up all worked hard, but upward mobility was rare, as was belief that something better was possible.

It takes *conscious*, intentional thought and action to become successful. It takes acceptance of risks and not being afraid to fail. It also takes an unyielding belief in yourself, your product or service, and a willingness to learn and be open to new ideas and thought. It starts with your having a clear definition of what success means to you. To be truly successful, you require more than just money.

Since I published my first book, I've had a lot of positive comments. I've also had the opportunity to work with some great companies as a direct result of business owners and CEOs reading *Bottom Line Focus*. When I go into an office and see a copy of my book on someone's desk with page markers, notes in the margins, and dog-eared pages, it is very gratifying.

Anyone who has published a book will agree that most people don't write primarily to sell copies. I authored *Bottom Line Focus* simply to differentiate myself as a coach who has been a CEO and business owner. I've faced many of the same problems and opportunities that many of you are facing today. From that perspective, the book was a big success because it resulted directly in some long-term engagements with some great companies and their management teams.

*Bottom Line Focus* was based largely on my own experiences working for a *Fortune* 500 company as well as my founding and running two companies after I decided to go on my own.

This book is enhanced by what I've learned working with numerous small- and midtier businesses over the past sixteen years.

The biggest difference between this volume and my previous one is that this book is primarily about *you*! Over the past sixteen years, I've had the privilege of working with numerous CEOs and business founders and owners. Many of them are at the point in life where they are thinking about transition plans.

Let's face it. There are only a few options for cashing out of a small- or midtier privately held company:

- Outright sale to a financial or strategic buyer
- Sale of stock-ownership plan to employees
- Turning it over to family members, possibly financing the sale for them by taking payments in retirement

No matter what you prefer, I think we will all agree it's great to have options and to get the best-possible valuations.

To develop your business for transition, you must create sustainable sales growth and profitability, which can continue without your hands-on involvement. That's the focus of this book, helping you identify what you want and developing your business to make it happen.

Through experience, I've designed a business-development process that has proven to generate results. But like any process, it's only as good as its execution.

Notice I said it's a process, not a plan or strategy document. It isn't meant to be static. The business environment is changing faster each year. If you can't understand and address those changes early, you're in trouble. History is littered with examples of companies that waited too long to meet market demands.

Kodak is a prime example. The company held numerous patents on digital photography, but its film business was generating huge profits. Kodak stayed committed to film and became a minor player in digital imaging.

Study mainframe computer makers in the 1980s, and you will find numerous examples. They were committed to large mainframes and infrastructure, and most of their revenue came from hardware sales and maintenance. They completely dismissed networked minicomputers such as those from DEC and Data General and paid the price. Most no longer exist. But, ignoring that lesson, the minicomputer makers themselves blew off networked PCs, and in about ten years, those companies were all gone.

This business-development process is a tool to help you review your business and its role in the market place on a regular basis. The goal is to keep abreast of potential, or pending, market changes, and how they may impact your situation with your current products and services.

You must have a clear vision of what you want and a timeframe to get there. But you must also be willing to take the needed, *conscious* actions to realize your goals.

What are your personal goals, ambitions, and dreams? Where do you see yourself and your family in the future? And what must your business do to get you there?

Most of us go into business with the idea of creating something valuable to provide for us in retirement and maybe to create something to leave for the next generation. Sadly, many of us wait until we're ready to transition before we start thinking about valuation and positioning the company for sale.

Some of my clients are business owners or shareholding CEOs, who have worked and invested time and capital in their businesses. Many are in their fifties and sixties and are beginning to think about what's next for them.

The common thread among these folks is that, many don't know and even more haven't thought about what's next. They are still immersed in the day-to-day operations with minimal thought of the future.

A few years ago, I was talking with the owner of an eight-figure business who'd had his company on and off the market several times. He said, "You know, when I want to sell my business nobody wants it. And when I don't everyone wants it."

He hadn't taken the time to develop his business into one that could demonstrate sustainable year-over-year growth and profitability. When times were good and the business was making money, he was satisfied. When he hit a downturn, he became interested in selling.

What he really wanted was to take out large amounts of cash in the good years, reinvest little back into the business, and sell when the business hit hard times. Obviously, that isn't a transition strategy that provides value to either the buyer or the seller. While this is an extreme example, I've learned that many business leaders haven't given a lot of thought to transition planning or maximizing the value of their business over the long term.

The process detailed in this book, which I've used successfully with my clients, will facilitate your path to doing just that. I hope it helps you to think differently about what's possible for your business and for you.

I've written a supplemental workbook, available free of charge to readers, to help you document your path. Each chapter aligns with a chapter in the workbook.

Download the free workbook here: http://www.bottomline-coach.com/bd-workbook.

# Introduction

Whether you think you can, or you think you
can't you're right.

—HENRY FORD

This quotation is short and to the point.
Success doesn't just happen. It's intentional. You either
choose to be successful or you don't. While I agree that none of
us starts out in business with the decision *not* to be successful,
the actions we take, or don't take, determine our results.

## FIRST, HOW DO WE DEFINE SUCCESS?
The *Merriam-Webster* dictionary defines it as "the fact of getting or achieving wealth, respect, or fame," but this interpretation
can't be complete. I've known hundreds of high-net-worth people
over the years. Frankly, very few of them seemed remotely happy.

Success means different things to each of us. I found a lot of
quotes from famous people that were wordy and presumptuous.
Success is what each of us perceives it to be. Over the years I
migrated to my own definition, it centers on peace of mind.

I believe that if you are at peace with yourself, you are successful. For me, peace of mind encompasses many things. To achieve it, I need enough wealth to live well and provide for my family. I need to be comfortable that I've done my best and left nothing on the table. Last but not least, I need to be OK with where I am spiritually. This is a definition I migrated to over the years, after having gone through many earlier versions.

Your definition could be quite different. That doesn't matter. What does matter is that you understand what it is, and don't keep trying to hit a moving target.

One of the things I ask my clients when we put a strategy in place is, "How will you measure success?" It's critical for you to define it for yourself somewhere in the process of reading this book and doing the exercises in the workbook.

Nearly everything that happens in life and in business is the result of the decisions you make, or don't make. Many of us are afraid to decide even when it's obvious that change needs to occur. *Inaction is simply a decision not to act.* Decisions are scary when you can't see the future and can't be certain of the outcome. Having complete confidence in yourself and in your plan makes things easier.

You must consciously think and take decisive action necessary to achieve whatever your definition of success is. It rarely happens on its own. What do I mean by *conscious* thinking?

Neuroscientists have conducted studies that have revealed that only about 5 percent to 10 percent of our cognitive activities are conscious (e.g., decisions, emotions, actions, behavior, etc.). The remaining 90 percent of our brain activity is generated in an unconscious manner. If you've failed at something in the past, your subconscious tells you to avoid that activity. If someone has told you that you lacked intelligence, your confidence in your decision-making ability is reduced. In fact, many of our earliest experiences are negative. "Don't touch that; don't eat that; don't talk to strangers." (That last warning is not being particularly useful if you are a salesperson!) Many of us carry that attitude our entire lives, always seeing the reasons why something can't be done.

So, if you already believe you can't be wealthy or successful, you are more likely not to be. You are more likely to accept things as they are. The first step is believing you can do whatever you want. Have a clear vision of what that is, and focus on the result.

## Conscious Focused Action Model - 1

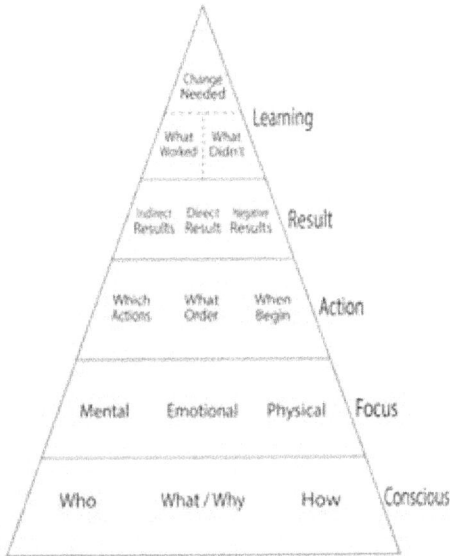

In his book, *The Conscious Millionaire*,[1] J. V. Crum III talks about a focused-action model. The illustration below from his book caught my attention.

---

1 J. V. Crum III, *Conscious Millionaire* (Conscious World Press, 2014).

As you can see, the basis for all deliberate action is consciousness. The what/ why that Crum shows at the base of the model is the vision you create. You then *consciously* follow the progression in the chart to a result. It makes me think how many of us start in the center. We take action—"reaction" might be a better term—and that activity provides a result, positive or negative. Reacting to what happens in your business is not the same as intentionally building long-term value.

This book will show you a clear path to building value in your organization, and creating personal wealth and satisfaction, through intentional action and sustainable business development. I hope it will also cause you to expand your thinking and to reach higher.

But learning a process is far different than executing it. The process I will discuss will be the vehicle, but you are the fuel that makes it run.

This book is about you—the seven- or eight-figure business owner or CEO. It is directed at giving you an opportunity to think differently, not only about your business but also about you and how you function within it.

You probably chose this book because you had an interest in creating more value in your business. Good! That's what we're going to explore together.

I remember when I first became a CEO. It was exciting and was something many of us, working in large corporations dreamed about. I remember my first business cards with the titles of president and CEO. What a great feeling! But then reality settled in.

I learned it wasn't nearly as much fun as I thought it would be. I saw an article on the website Small Business Trends[2] that I found to

---

2 Scott Shane, "Learning by Doing and Entrepreneurship," Small Business Trends, https://smallbiztrends.com/2015/06/learning-by-doing-entrepreneurship.html.

fit my situation exactly. When they conducted a survey, 51 percent of the people who were asked, "What's the best way to learn more about entrepreneurship?" responded with this: "Start a company."

What a perfect description of my journey.

Well, I did it. I put job security and every dollar I had on the line and took the plunge. I didn't know what I didn't know! We grew to about $50 million in sales with over six hundred employees in the United States and Europe. And as the quote says, most of what I learned was after I was committed.

That commitment, along with the belief that I could not fail, allowed me to beat the odds. Generally, about 50 percent of start-up businesses fail in their first four years, but mine wasn't among them.

If you're a business owner your life is tied to your business. It's not like working for someone else, in which case where you can leave your problems in your office. When you are a CEO, you live those problems, and so does your family. That's part of what you signed up for when you decided to become an entrepreneur. You have learned firsthand that "if it were easy everyone would do it."

It can also be a rewarding path both financially and personally. According to an article on the *business know-how* website, the US Census Bureau reports that there are more than 27 million business in the United States, and only 655,587, or 2.5 percent, have 20 or more employees. About 18,500 have 500 employees or more.[3] Only about 4 percent have over $1 million in annual sales. Obviously, success is hard to achieve. You must have a plan. You must believe in that plan. You must execute that plan. This

---

3 Janet Attard, "How Much Do Small Businesses Really Earn?" January 9, 2017, https://www.businessknowhow.com/money/earn.htm.

challenge begins and ends with you, the small- or midtier business owner or CEO.

Who else will drive of our economy? Certainly not the government. It redistributes wealth, but creates no value on its own. Large corporations no longer show allegiance to any country and now consider themselves global. With few exceptions, most don't worry about the communities they inhabit or the people who live there. Rather they are concerned about lower labor costs, reducing taxes, and pleasing the stock market with their quarterly earnings. So, to a large degree, economic growth depends on you, the small- or midtier business owner or CEO.

It's an awesome responsibility. But if you don't do it, who will? Those who succeed can reap huge rewards. And it can be done!

As I said earlier, my first company grew from a start-up to nearly $50 million dollars in annual sales. We had 550 employees in the United States and over 100 in Europe. We also had in excess of $1 million per month in payroll. Most of that money went right back into the local economies where our facilities were located.

The good news in all of this isn't just for you CEOs. When you strengthen your businesses, you can reap real wealth for your employees as well as yourselves and your families. While building that wealth for yourself, you are helping to rebuild your communities.

My goal with this book is to make you aware of a proven business-development process that can provide for sustainable growth year over year. But in addition to the process, I want to generate thought through the accompanying workbook and open your mind to new possibilities. Perhaps by helping you I'm helping my grandchildren enjoy the opportunities that I've had.

When I ran my companies, I was alone. If I didn't understand something, or had a problem there was really no one to ask. I couldn't admit to my staff or investors that I wasn't clear on a subject or was unsure of what to do. They looked to me for confidence and leadership.

I became a coach because I want to be that person who I needed back then. I developed the process we'll review through fifteen years as a midtier company CEO and sixteen years as a business coach. I've been involved with hundreds of companies and have learned what they did well and where many were lacking.

I've also created a business-development process workbook available for download on my website at http://www.bottomline-coach.com/bd-workbook.

The workbook is a template in which you can add notes and answer questions after each chapter to help you facilitate your path to success. The download is a supplement to this book and is available without charge.

# Section 1: Leadership

One

# It Starts and Ends with You

> Only three things happen naturally in organizations: friction, confusion, and underperformance. Everything else requires leadership.
>
> —PETER DRUCKER

A s I said at the beginning, this book is about *you*. When you are the owner or CEO everything starts or ends with you. We discussed how many opportunities are available to you as the person in charge. But ultimately all of the responsibility rests on you as well.

Therefore, the success of any business-development plan, any strategic plan, or any change initiative also depends on you. That isn't to say that you do it all personally of course, but I find many executives trying to do just that. The success of your organization relies on you being an effective leader. So, before we get into the strategy and execution of a business-development effort, we would be remiss if we didn't begin with leadership.

## A CONCEPT OF LEADERSHIP

Warren Bennis is quoted as saying, "Leadership is the capacity to translate vision into reality." Neither vision nor leadership can be successful without the other.

What is effective leadership? There are as many answers to this question as there are excuses for failure. If I look back at my working life and think of great leaders, what comes to mind first is that I've known so few. I've met hundreds of managers, but just a few great leaders. As is often said, "Assets are to be managed; people are to be led."

I think one of the main failures I've seen in leaders is their inability to keep the workforce engaged in the work they're doing. Employee engagement in the United States is said to be lower than 20 percent. That's correct; according to a Gallup poll, 84 percent of employees are not engaged in their work.[4] The same study stated that employers with highly engaged workforces outperform their peers by 147 percent in earnings per share. Another study by Dale Carnegie and MSW Research gave additional facts[5]:

- Eleven billion dollars is lost annually due to employee turnover
- Companies with engaged employees outperform their competitors by 202 percent
- Forty-five percent of employees are not engaged at all

---

4 Susan Sorenson, "How Employee Engagement Drives Growth," *Gallup News*, June 20, 2013, http://news.gallup.com/businessjournal/163130/employee-engagement-drives-growth.aspx.

5 "Engaged Employees Infographic," Dale Carnegie Training, https://www.dalecarnegie.com/employee-engagement/engaged-employees-infographic/.

- Twenty-six percent are *actively disengaged*
- Twenty-nine percent are engaged

What is the root cause of the lack of engagement? My experience says it's directly related to lack of effective leadership.

Of course, none of us are poor leaders. At least I've never heard anyone admit to being an ineffective leader. The problem I hear most often is that "*they* don't get it" or "*they* aren't committed." Both of these, of course, are leadership issues.

The employee-engagement statistics shouldn't be surprising. If those employers don't have a clear idea of where they are going and the belief that they can get there, they resort to a week-to-week strategy or in worse cases a day-to-day strategy. You must clearly define and document what *it* is that they don't get.

- If employees are given confusing directions, of course they'll perform poorly.
- If they're presented with expectations that are undocumented and constantly changing, of course they'll get frustrated.
- If they don't have well-defined goals, of course they'll lack motivation.
- If they're not held accountable to agreed-upon metrics, of course they'll tend to slack off.
- If they're not respected and treated equally as members of teams, of course they'll become disengaged.

The good news is that leaders are made not born. You can learn to be an effective leader, but it starts with confidence and belief in yourself.

How do you start?

- Do you regularly take the time to really listen?
- Are you available and approachable?
- Do you and your employees have a sense that "we're all in this together"?
- Are you in a habit of praising others for their accomplishments?
- Do you celebrate your successes as a team?
- Do you actively promote a team spirit throughout your organization?
- Are you visible? Do your employees see you on the plant floor or in the warehouse?

A great leader has a vision, communicates that vision relentlessly, builds a great team to achieve that vision, and removes any obstacles that might impede that team.

General Colin Powell summed it up well in the following statement: *"The day soldiers stop bringing you their problems is the day you have stopped leading them. They have either lost confidence that you can help them or concluded that you do not care. Either case is a failure of leadership."*

To be an effective leader of others you must first learn to lead yourself. You must be accountable to others if you want them to be accountable to you. This requires *conscious* action on your part each and every day. Know what you want to accomplish, communicate that vision to all stakeholders, and be accountable for results. Accepting excuses for anything other than quantified results weakens your vision and leadership role.

Things will happen every day to impede your progress. How you deal with these things that decides whether you're an effective leader. The examples above are just that, examples. Part of every major decision you make has to include its impact on your customers as well as your employees. People respond better when they are valued as part of a team.

Is that important? The fact is most impediments to business success can be directly attributed to people. I know, that the assumption has always been that it isn't people, it's process. I disagree. People are responsible to define, document, measure, revise (if necessary), and adhere to the process. But first they have to understand clearly what the end result of the process is, and why it's important.

Your ability to attract, challenge, and retain excellent people will determine the success of your business. If your employees love your company, your customers will as well. What are your employees saying about you and the company when they speak to others inside as well as outside the workplace?

There are hundreds of books written on leadership and the various approaches to take to be a better leader. I'm not going to discuss them here. This book is about getting you to think about your leadership style, the results you're getting, and what you need to *consciously* do to improve.

## TRANSFORMING THE ORGANIZATION
How do you define transformation as it pertains to your company? There are a number of areas in most small- and midtier companies that are potential targets for transformation. The obvious ones are quality, customer service, growth, and profitability, to name a few. My thinking is that true transformation begins with people and culture.

Again, transformation begins and ends with leadership. A leader is responsible for defining the culture of an organization, and *consciously* cultivating that culture. Saying it isn't enough. You have to walk the talk.

If your employees feel that you don't listen or don't care, they are unlikely to highlight problems and provide suggestions. They are also unlikely to have ownership of the impact of the problems on the products or customers.

To succeed with any change initiative or strategy, you must

- clarify and document where you want to be;
- realistically understand where you are currently and take a hard look at how you got there;
- take an objective look at your leadership-team members and discern whether they are willing and able to carry the culture and change initiatives forward;
- have ways to measure progress and trends;
- have a clear definition of success; and
- *consciously* communicate with and motivate your team members. Educate them about why this transformation is important, and about how it will affect them, and your customers.

Perhaps the most important component of transformation is your belief and commitment, and how well you show that commitment every day. If you aren't openly dedicated to change, I can assure you no one else will be.

To transform an organization, you must also be able to attract and retain excellent people. They must understand your vision, become excited about it, and commit to achieving it.

Human resource development may be the most critical goal of any organization today. It's simply harder to find and hire great people.

According to a US Department of Labor report, only about 63 percent of working-age adults are participating in the workforce. Depending on the time of year, another 4.5 percent are unemployed and looking for work. That leaves about 33 percent self-employed, or not looking for employment.[6]

You sell your products and services to your market. You must also think about how you can sell the benefits of working for your company to the prospective workforce.

That's a radically different idea than what we're used to, but it's a fact of life. Our potential employees are more knowledgeable these days and have more information available to them to make career decisions. In addition, we must somehow tap into the 33 percent that aren't currently available to us.

Employee turnover has always been costly. But in this environment, it's even more so. Losing a key employee can result in an extended search to find a comparable replacement. This is another area where leadership is critical. People don't leave great companies; they leave poor managers or leaders. According to Gallup polls, 50 percent of employees who quit cite their manager as a reason.[7]

Employee turnover is a huge problem, but perhaps employees remaining on the job while being disengaged is a bigger problem. You are paying their salaries[8] and benefits but not getting an acceptable return on your investment. Leadership and management play a huge roll here as well. An article by Jack Altman in Forbes online, dated February 22, 2017, is entitled "Don't Be Surprised When Your Employees Quit." It shows a direct correlation between management and turnover. The following chart from

---

6 United States Department of Labor website, January 12, 2018, https://data.bls.gov/timeseries/LNS11300000.

7 Benjamin Snyder, "Half of Us Quit Our Jobs Because of Bad Bosses," *Fortune*, April 2, 2015, http://fortune.com/2015/04/02/quit-reasons/.

8 Jack Altman, "Don't be Surprised When Your Employees Quit," *Forbes*, February 22, 2017, https://www.forbes.com/sites/valleyvoices/2017/02/22/dont-be-surprised-when-your-employees-quit/ - 4b7d40ba325e.

**I feel I can approach my manager
with any type of questions.**

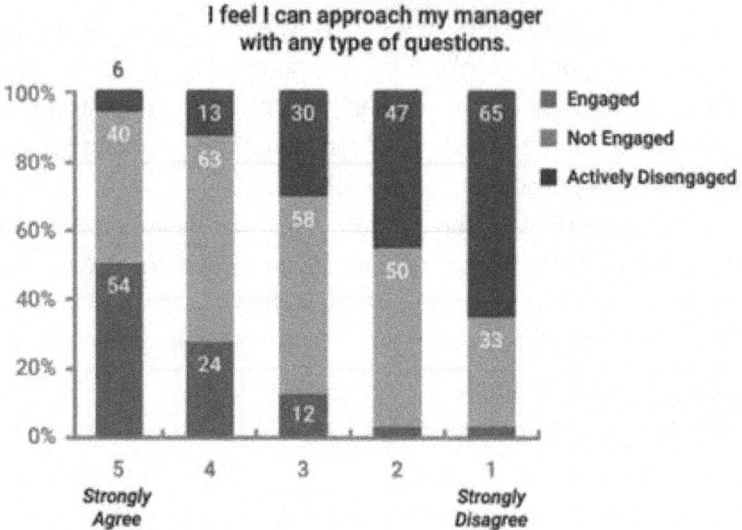

that article illustrates employee engagement is directly proportional to management effectiveness.

Two points are critical.

1. The organizations that will be consistently successful in attracting and retaining great people will require great leadership.
2. The successful transformation of any organization is dependent on your ability to attract and lead excellent people.

## LEADERSHIP AND COMMUNICATIONS

"Communicate" is an action verb.

When I founded my first company, I started with just two employees. For the first few years, as the company grew rapidly,

I could maintain a close personal relationship with most employees. I knew practically everyone by name. As I walked through the facility, it was not uncommon for someone to stop me and tell me about an issue or a success story I hadn't been directly involved with.

As we grew to more than six hundred employees, I became increasingly isolated from the day-to-day activities. We were developing layers of management, and I was afraid we were turning into one of those impersonal monsters I had left years earlier.

So I decided to make a *conscious* effort to communicate more effectively. We held all-hands meetings every six months to review our strategic goals and our performance. These were typically one-way sessions, since most people were reluctant to speak up in such large groups.

One day our human-resources director suggested that each month I invite twelve to fifteen randomly selected employees to a "breakfast with the CEO." She felt that they would appreciate the chance to ask questions and give input.

Initially, I flinched at the idea. I wasn't comfortable with the notion that I, as the CEO, was so special that people should be excited to come in early and have breakfast with me. But I made a *conscious* decision to go along with her suggestion, and it turned out to be one of the best communication tools I've ever used. Every month those fifteen people went back to their workstations and communicated there as well.

People felt comfortable in this small-group atmosphere and opened up with ideas and comments. It really seemed to help cement the idea that we were "all in this together." We continued this practice for the duration of my time as CEO. The message is that you must *consciously* ask yourself where, why, and how you can actively communicate your vision through all levels of your organization.

Later in this book, we'll talk about the mechanics of how to do develop and execute your business-development process, but the belief and communication rests with you.

If you don't believe in your vision and communicate that belief to all of your stakeholders, the process simply won't happen. Lack of leadership, commitment, and accountability are some of the major reasons that change initiatives fail.

## CHAPTER SUMMARY

- Leadership, communications, and employee engagement starts and ends with you. If you aren't consciously working to improve these areas, no one else will.
- Hiring and retaining engaged employees are critical to your success.
- Communications is filtered from the CEO to lower levels of the organization. Make sure your message is being heard.

Answer the leadership questions in the workbook at http://www.bottomlinecoach.com/bd-workbook.

Two

# Core Values

Customers will never love a company until the
employees love it first.

—Simon Sinek, author of *Start with Why*

There are numerous books on organizational culture. On Amazon.com if you do a search on those two words, you will see about seventeen pages of results.

If you do a Google search on the same term, you are likely to get over three million results. Clearly, culture is the new buzz word for business.

One definition I found stated, "Organizational culture is defined as the underlying beliefs, assumptions, values, and ways of interacting that contribute to the unique social and psychological environment of an organization."

That's probably an accurate definition, but it may be confusing and somewhat wordy if you want to build a strategy around it. I think the quote above from Simon Sinek sums things up well; if employees love your company, that will be reflected in everything they do. Customers will react to their attitudes in a positive way. It works the same way when employees hate their jobs. Customers see those attitudes as well, through poor quality, missed ship dates, and poor customer relations. They will in turn react to your company in a negative way.

To me culture is having your employees understand your strategy and value proposition, believe it, believe in you, and do the right things when no one is looking. They should see your customers as their own and be motivated and compensated to provide excellent results consistently.

One of the ways to drive this ownership is to have a set of core values that are nonnegotiable. Almost every company I've been associated with has a set of stated core values on a plaque somewhere. It usually includes things like integrity, fairness, excellence, innovation, quality, or similar words that turn out to be just words. When I begin to dig into how the company actually works, all too often I find that one or more of these values have been compromised numerous times due to "special" circumstances. If one of your core values is fairness, but you don't treat everyone the same, what does that tell your employees?

One client I've been associated with for about six years has a core value abbreviated as SQp. Safety, Quality, productivity with the first two words capitalized to emphasize the importance of each. He has a daily roll-call meeting with each shift, and he has a standing deal with his employees. If he fails to mention SQp in the first five minutes and they catch it, he gives each of them $100. He has in fact, purposely avoided using it on several occasions and paid the money. The message he sends here far outweighs the cost of the cash payment, it says he is serious and that those values are nonnegotiable.

If you have core values posted somewhere in your facility, and you don't live by them relentlessly all the time, take them down. They are telling your employees you don't mean what you say.

So what are your core values? Quality is a given in today's environment. If you don't have it, social media will tell the world. Integrity and fairness are great values to have and now should be nonnegotiable if you hope to attract and retain excellent people.

Something simple like, "Treat everyone like you'd want to be treated" can make a huge impact on customers and employees. That's a value that can be demonstrated to employees, and carried forward to your customers. But you have to be consistent.

Core values should be tied to strategy. They should mean something to your customers and to your employees. If these two entities buy into your standards and know that you are consistent in keeping them as well. Such values can be very powerful.

Innovation is a core value that all companies should consider incorporating. Because the world is changing at an accelerated rate, new ideas for products and services are critical. But to truly foster a culture of innovation, you must allow for failure without repercussions. If you allow all of your employees the freedom to present new ideas, that aren't dismissed without discussion, and offer incentives for implementation you will foster innovation. Allowing failure without ridicule and repercussion is just as important.

The take away here is that you should make core values meaningful, communicate them, and be accountable for upholding them if you expect others to do the same. That takes a *conscious* effort on your part and on the part of your management team.

## CHAPTER SUMMARY

- Say what you mean, and mean what you say.
- Be consistent with your stated values across all levels of the organization.
- Your organizational culture is visible externally as well as internally; make it a good one.

Go to the workbook and complete the exercise on values: http://www.bottomlinecoach.com/bd-workbook.

# Section 2: Strategy

Three

# Vision


> If you limit your choices only to what seems
> possible or reasonable, you disconnect yourself
> from what you truly want, and all that is left is a
> compromise.

—Robert Fritz

## PERSONAL VISION

The quote above is very accurate. Most of us have a general idea of wanting to do something at some point in the future. Too often, the picture we form in our mind is self-limiting. The question isn't what you think you can attain, it should be what do you want to attain?

What do you want out of life? This might seem like an easy question until you really think about it. Many of us are middle aged and don't know the answer, so we adjust what we want, to fit "reality." In truth, reality is what we *consciously* choose it to be, either through action or failure to act.

One of the first things I ask a prospective client is what he or she wants to achieve on a personal level in the next five to ten years. Some have an answer for that. The next question is this: Do you know what your business must do to allow you to do that? The percentage of clients with clear answers to the second question is smaller than the first. The third question after receiving an answer to number two is this: Do you know what you need to accomplish to get your business to the stage at which you can achieve your personal goals? Getting clear, crisp answers to all three is a rarity indeed.

We are all self-limiting to a point. How often do you think of doing something and the first thoughts are negative? It won't work because it's different or risky, or any one of a million other restrictive thoughts. Over the years, I've become very interested in consciousness and mindfulness. I've done a lot of reading on the subjects and thought about how consciousness has impacted my life. I guess I really didn't know the technical terms associated with positive thinking and never thought about it until later in life. When I look back and examine the many things that I've done over the years, it really hit me. I've often followed the *conscious* path but unconsciously. I know that makes no sense but hear me out. I had a clear understanding of what needed to be done, and I was absolutely convinced that I could make it happen not that it was easy because it wasn't.

But I always believed in myself and my work ethic; I took the risks and made it happen. What I lacked in many cases was a clear vision. I was often my own worst enemy; since I didn't have a clear vision, I never allowed myself to declare success. I didn't take the time to clarify what success looked like.

I also had a belief that what I was doing made sense. I had no doubt that I would succeed. A large part of my business's growth and success was because I took risks, and then committed myself to make them pay off. I went out on more than a few limbs, and thankfully only a few broke. *Consciously* believing in your vision and committing yourself to making things happen is critical to success.

Based on my personal experience and on hundreds of conversations with business owners as a coach, it's apparent that most business owners and CEOs lack a clear vision. And those who do have one, limit themselves to striving for something based on what they've done in the past. Our vision of our future is based on past performance. It's rare and refreshing to see someone think big or different!

Your company's vision should be built around what you want to achieve personally. Do you want to retire at a certain age? Do you want to continue working at a reduced role? Do you want to turn management over to someone else and take monthly cash payments? Will you choose a family member or an outside manager? Do you want to sell outright? How much cash will you need to realize your personal vision? When will you need it? Answers to these questions will determine what your company needs to accomplish, in what timeframe, and what investments you'll need to make.

The point isn't that we don't know the answers to these questions; it's that we rarely think about them until we're forced to by some circumstance. We spend so much time and energy with day-to-day activates that we seldom think *consciously* about the future.

You should always have your business in a position to sell it. The time to prepare for transition is not six months or a year before you are ready to make the move. Being ready to sell, does not mean you're selling. It means that you have maximized the value of your business and have provided several great options on how you want to move forward.

Let's look at some facts about business valuations. I read an article in the *New York Times* website entitled "Do You Really Expect Your Business to Get You through Retirement?" The author presented a hypothetical sale as an illustration. I thought it was an excellent example. Let's say your company is close to the following example:

| | |
|---|---|
| Annual sales | $10 million |
| EBITDA | $1 million |
| Sales price or 4.5 times EBITDA | $4.5 million |
| Taxes and expenses of sale 35% | $1.757 million |
| Net proceeds from the sale | $2.925 million |

If that money was invested at 4 percent it would provide a pre-tax annual income of about $117,000. Remember that you, as the owner, had been enjoying about $1 million in annual cash flow running a going concern.[9]

Back to the original questions: What do you want? When? What resources will you need?

## ORGANIZATIONAL VISION

Businesses typically plan by looking backward. They begin with historical performance and base future plans on some improvement of that. The focus is on doing more of the same, better. Leaders look to defend and extend current products and services, and place little emphasis on looking forward with new products and services.

---

9 Josh Patrick, "Do You Really Expect Your Business to Get You Through Retirement?," *New York Times.com*, September 20, 2010, https://boss.blogs.nytimes.com/2012/09/20/do-you-really-expect-your-business-to-get-you-through-retirement/.

Whether our visions are for our companies or for our personal lives, too many of us are in a wait and see modes. We all need to be in proactive modes. The reluctance to think big is due to the fact that many of us lack the confidence and belief in ourselves to drive the businesses to achieve their highest potential.

As I have mentioned, I probably didn't have a clear vision when I started my first business. I knew what markets I'd compete in, and I knew my target customers, but I never dreamed it would grow to the level it did. But I had a good understanding of the market and the problem I set out to solve. And I did have a solid, unique value proposition. My vision was limited to short-term goals: make it through the first year, make some money, and develop a market presence. In short, my vision for the first few years was simply surviving another year? How many of us never get past that thinking?

I worked with a midsize company for a few years, as a consultant/coach. This company was very profitable and revenue was about $50 million annually. Despite the excellent margins, or maybe because of them, the problems were numerous.

The company had a huge concentration of revenue in a single account, and really didn't commit to make any investment to offset that problem. The worst happened: the company lost its huge account, revenue decreased significantly, and the executives were scrambling. The reason I mention them here is that the majority shareholder and chairman, made the comment at the beginning of this book. He said, "You know when I want to sell my company, nobody wants to buy it; when I don't want to sell everyone wants it." When times were good, he and the management team reaped the benefits of huge bonuses and profit sharing; when things got tough, he looked for a buyer, and there were no takers. He didn't have a clear vision of what he wanted. So his management team's vision became maximizing profits in the short term to maximize profit-sharing checks. I'm not sure where the company is today, but it's the best example I can think of to illustrate my point. This company knew for at least five years that the risk of losing a single account could have a catastrophic impact. But lack of a clear vision, a reluctance to strategically address the problem, and *consciously* act allowed the worst to happen.

The answer is that you should always have your company ready to sell. If your vision is to sell in five years, the time to develop value in your company is now. If you want to maximize the value of your company, you need to show historical and repeatable growth year over year.

One of the things I see quite often is that even if the owner gets a price he or she can live with, the transaction still doesn't provide a happy ending. The owner may be asked to stay on for a time to work with the new owner, or the buyer may ask that he or she take a percentage of his or her selling price as part of future earnings. If the buyer isn't convinced that the business is able to generate sustainable earnings after you leave, a prudent buyer may require future participation on your part.

You need a clear vision and you must *consciously* communicate that vision to all stakeholders. But communicating it isn't enough; you have to live it.

What is your vision for your company over the next five years? What markets will you serve? What products or services will you offer? What can you do to provide real value to your customers while creating revenue opportunities for your company? What will you do to make it tough for your customers to move to a competitor? How can you create a niche that you can dominate?

For our purposes, we aren't interested yet in developing a clever statement; we are interested in painting a picture of what we want the company to look like in five years. For example, consider the following:

- We want to reach $50 million in sales.
- A vision of no customer makes up more than 10 percent of revenue.
- The company will be a market leader in turnkey solutions to customer problems by providing X.
- We want to develop management depth.
- We want to develop a new product or service that has a strong market advantage.

Remember this quote:

> Good leaders must communicate vision clearly, creatively, and continually. However, the vision doesn't come alive until the leader models it.
>
> —JOHN C. MAXWELL

This book is designed to offer you a new way to look at your organization and develop a business-development strategy that builds value.

But to get your full attention, we need to make it personal. What do you want from your business? In what timeframe? What is your personal situation today? What do you need your business to provide to allow you to realize your goals?

## CHAPTER SUMMARY

Your personal vision should impact your organizational vision. Be clear about what you want to do and when, and develop your organization to achieve that.

Your future is in your hands, you have more control than you might think.

Build value and develop options early rather than later.

Have your business ready to sell well before you are ready to sell.

Don't limit your vision for the future by looking back.

Take some time to answer the questions in your free workbook to begin developing your business to meet your goals. The workbook is available here at http://www.bottomlinecoach.com/bd-workbook.

## WARNING!

If you aren't committed to success and willing to look deep inside at the core reasons you aren't as successful as you think you should be, then this book may not be for you. Part of the process involves an honest evaluation of your company as it exists today, and how you function as a leader. If you are unable or unwilling to do this and *consciously* commit to action, this will be just another exercise.

Four

# Where Are You Now?

Nothing stops an organization faster than people
who believe that the way you worked yesterday is
the best way to work tomorrow.

—Jon Madonna

I recently read a book by Adam Hartung entitled *Create
Marketplace Disruption*.[10]

It's an excellent book and looks at the reasons most of the
Fortune 1000 and even Fortune 500 companies from twenty
years ago are no longer on the lists. For example, of the S&P 500
in 1955, only 74 or 15 percent exist today. Since 1962, of the one
thousand largest companies by sales in the United States, only
160 or 16 percent managed to stay in that group. Hartung provides some historical analysis of some of them and it's very well
written. Two things that are very clear:

---

10 Adam Hartung, *Create Marketplace Disruption* (FT Press, 2009).

- All companies run through growth cycles, and eventually hit sales plateaus.
- Once they reach the revenue stall point, three out of four experience negative growth, and in fact begin a persistent decline. In other words, after revenue stalls, they don't recover.

One of the sections of Hartung's book that resonated with me included the phrase "defend and extend." Hartung states, "The focus still remains largely on how to do better what was previously done. Business education is steeped in optimizing execution as opposed to managing innovation. This focus fit the business world's needs from 1940 into the 1980s well, but times have changed. Markets are now global, and they have become increasingly dynamic."

It's the thinking that exists in many of our businesses today. Rather than address market requirements and competitive conditions early, many companies are tied to their current infrastructures, technologies, and products. Realigning to meet new market requirements could make many of their current assets obsolete, so they continue to focus on "how to do better what they've previously done." When revenue plateaus they cut costs, reduce overhead such (as R&D), and mortgage their futures.

The following chart is a modified version of one in Hartung's book. It clearly illustrates the growth stages and the risks associated with growth as well as stagnation.

This scenario is very common and widespread. Hartung gives several historical examples of large business failures that followed the defend-and-extend concept, but it isn't just large business that fall into that trap.

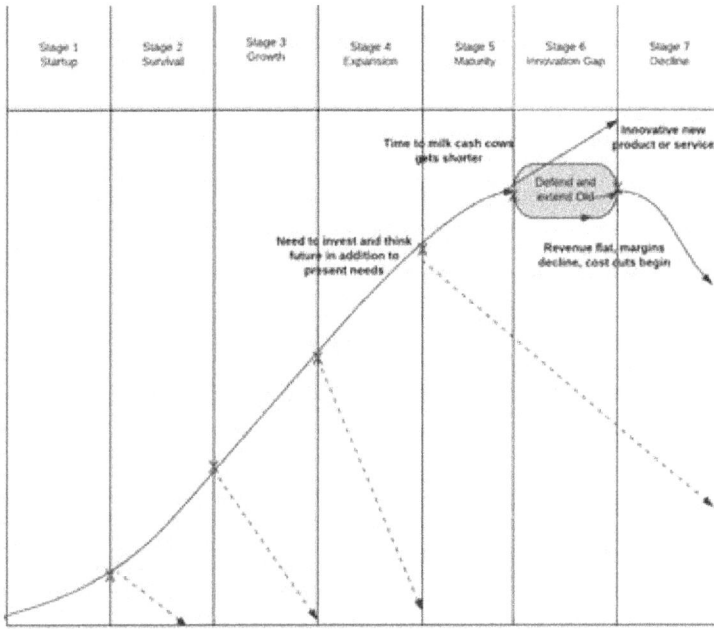

| Stage 1 Startup | Stage 2 Survival | Stage 3 Growth | Stage 4 Expansion | Stage 5 Maturity | Stage 6 Innovation Gap | Stage 7 Decline |

Time to milk cash cows gets shorter

Innovative new product or service

Defend and extend Old

Need to invest and think future in addition to present needs

Revenue flat, margins decline, cost cuts begin

X  Potential chaos point

So, when you honestly evaluate where you are now, consider what you're doing from an innovation perspective and what you should be doing from a market perspective. What are your competitors doing? How has your market changed? How do you compare?

I've been involved in numerous acquisitions and mergers from my own companies to client companies. There are many things that come up during due diligence that adversely affect a company's valuation. I've seen many of these in client organizations. Items like:

- High concentration of revenue in one or two accounts
- Lack of documented systems and processes

- Lack of management depth (This is especially common when the founder is running the business; the success of the business depends on him or her remaining with the organization.)
- Lack of a compelling value proposition (a differentiator)
- A historical rollercoaster of sales and profits
- Lack of, or obsolete, infrastructure
- Product or service no longer meets market requirements

These items must be objectively identified, documented, and corrected.

## START WITH A SWOT

This is a simple tool to document and prioritize actions to either take full advantage of new opportunities or correct issues that may hinder growth. It's a quick visual reminder of where you are at a point in time. Notice that I said, "At a point in time." To be of real value, this should be a tool that's reviewed and updated on at least an annual basis.

Evaluate your organization internally:

## STRENGTHS

What real strengths does your company have in your market? They are only real strengths if your customers understand them, and agree that they do indeed add value for them. Some examples follow:

- Do you have manufacturing technology that guarantees the highest quality product and keeps the price competitive?

- Do you have proven results in a specific area that exceeds expectations in your market?
- Do you have a product or service that's superior to the competition and do your customers understand its value?
- Do you have exceptional human resources? For example, a top sales performer or an excellent technical resource. Counting people as among your strengths is a double-edged sword. If you have excellent technical resources or strong sales and marketing personnel, they are valuable to you. But they also create their own value in the marketplace and can quickly jump ship for a better deal. Processes and technologies that don't rely on specific people are the real answer.

## WEAKNESSES

Some examples of weaknesses follow:

- Management depth: Do you have the right people, in the right jobs to handle growth and increased responsibility?
- Is your company's success dependent on you personally?
- Do you have adequate access to credit or investment to facilitate growth?
- Are your products or services currently meeting or exceeding market expectations?
- Do you have technology or customer relationships that are tied to key people? If the person leaves, the knowledge or relationship leaves as well.

Then you should evaluate your position externally, by looking at your products or services, your market, and your competitors.

## OPPORTUNITIES

What opportunities are available now? Some examples follow:

- Is a competitor having quality or service issues?
- Has your market changed in a manner that is advantageous for you?
- Can you change the market through innovation?
- Can you move your products or services to new additional markets?
- Can you update your products or services and move ahead of the competition?
- Are there major companies in your industry, or a complementary industry with which you could create a mutually beneficial joint venture?

## THREATS

What are the major threats to your business? Some examples:

- Scarcity of qualified labor?
- Scarcity of special skills?
- High health care costs?
- New competition in the market?
- A major market shift (think Amazon and brick-and-mortar retailers)?

Be honest with yourself because other people will see these items, and it's better to address them first.

I've read articles that argue as to whether a SWOT evaluation is of any lasting value. My answer is that it depends on how you use it. Used properly it's a visual indicator of where you stand on achievement of your critical goals. But as things change, goals are completed, or products or markets change, it must be updated.

One of the major problems with doing a SWOT analysis within a management team (and without using an outside facilitator) is fear of honest and open debate. Too often the discussion is aligned with what the CEO or owner thinks. This is especially true if this person is the founder of the business.

If the management team is uncomfortable challenging assumptions and the CEO isn't open to fresh looks at the organization internally and externally, you're starting from a bad baseline. Your business development plan will be built on a poor foundation.

## CHAPTER SUMMARY

- Defend and extend is not a viable strategy for long-term value.
- Invest in innovation before you have to and before you reach the innovation gap.
- Be honest and critical in your internal and external assessment, or you are building on a weak foundation.
- Allow open discussion, or hire an outsider to facilitate the process.
- Some strengths can turn into weaknesses quickly.

I've included a worksheet in the companion workbook that you've downloaded to help you analyze and document each category: http://www.bottomlinecoach.com/bd-workbook.

Five

# Your Value Proposition

If you don't have a competitive advantage, don't
compete.

—Jack Welch

**W**hat is a value proposition, and why do you need one?
Simply put, it's the answer to one question, "With all the
products or services available to your customers in your market,
why should they buy from you?"

All sales opportunities come from a customer's want or need.
Once a customer decides that they want or need a product, all
sales decisions come down to two things: value and price. If you
can't answer the question above with a compelling reason, you're
viewed as a "me too." If you are perceived as the same as everyone else it all comes down to price. That may be OK if you are and
can remain the lowest cost provider. But it opens the door to a
larger company or offshore suppliers pricing you out of the market. Why buy a business, if you can make a competitor disappear?
The strengths and opportunities you documented in chapter 4
will help you create your unique value proposition.

A great example of changing your business to create value is one of my current clients.

This client owns a rubber-compounding-and-mixing company. Rubber mixing is a very mature market, and it's one in which you might not expect an opportunity to change the overall industry exists. But innovation isn't just limited to tech companies.

At one time, there were hundreds of mixing companies in the United States that operated outside the tire business. Over the past ten years, a large company has been consolidating the market. With the company's strong market position and buying power, it was driving prices down and eliminating the competition. My client, and others, had been forced to sell their products strictly on lowest price. My client had several offers to buy the company, at prices that didn't reflect the company's real value.

Several years ago, we developed a strategy that was unique in their industry. The company's executive team recognized that much of the chemical and engineering talent in this industry was aging, and too few people were entering the industry in technical positions. They decided they would reverse the common business model prevalent in the industry. Whereas most companies provided just enough technical resources to support their mixing businesses, the CEO decided this company would invest in technical skills and resources to make them their primary differentiator. Their mixing operation would become an added service to their technical offerings. They decided that new product development and the development of solutions for new elastomeric applications would become their target market. The company's ability to rapidly develop new products and devise application-based test environments has led to several new opportunities, one being a huge subsea project with a major oil company.

My client is also working with another major oil tool company as an outside resource to its own research and development organization. This has led to development of several products for them. In addition, a multi-billion-dollar foreign company hired a consulting firm to evaluate rubber manufacturers in the United States for possible collaboration. Of over three hundred evaluated, my client's company is in the final few with which the foreign company is talking with for potential collaboration. The client's company is one of the smallest being considered, but it is the one unique in the mix. Talks with this large multinational company have validated my client's strategic direction.

*The client's value proposition is based on delivering the optimum solution to elastomeric applications with the shortest time from development to market in the industry.*

Another example was my own company. I had been tasked to resolve a problem for the *Fortune* 500 company for which I was working. My partner and I saw an opportunity. If this company had the problem, chances were that others had it too. We developed a comprehensive software package to solve the logistics problem. Although we were a small start-up, we outsourced logistics functions for a dozen of the largest high-tech companies in the United States and Europe. We grew to be a midtier company and made the *Inc.* 500 list of America's fastest-growing companies. We accomplished all this despite our being a start-up with little balance-sheet strength.

Our value proposition was this: "*We use information to streamline processes that optimize inventory asset levels.*"

We understood our target market and what issues our potential customers were concerned with, and we addressed those issues directly.

A few years ago, I read a quote from someone you may have heard of. Bill Gates said, "The most meaningful way to differentiate your company from your competitors, the best way to put distance between you and the crowd is to do an outstanding job with information. How you gather, manage, and use information will determine whether you win or lose."

That's exactly what we did at our logistics company. We didn't charge for the use of our proprietary information technology; we included it as part of our standard services. We also weren't the low-price provider. We didn't compete on price, we offered real value in asset reduction. We didn't sell our intellectual property; we kept it proprietary even though we had numerous organizations wanting to buy it. We decided we didn't want to be a software company, but we did want to be the best in value-added logistics. Our technology provided us the opportunity to do that. You must pick a niche, be the best in that niche, and be constantly aware of potential market changes to remain the best.

Taking the time to develop a compelling value proposition is one way to build sustainable value in your business.

So what is it? It's a differentiator that sets you apart from the competition. It adds value to your customers that they recognize and agree with. Thinking that you have a great value proposition is unimportant unless your customer understands it and agrees with it.

How can you provide added value to your product or service in your market that makes you the obvious choice? It should be compelling enough that your customer considers price as an afterthought because they understand they are gaining so much value from what you do and how you do it. Your pricing should be competitive, but you should not necessarily be forced to compete on lowest purchase price.

As we will learn later in this book, your compelling UVP will become the focus of your marketing and sales efforts.

## CHAPTER SUMMARY

- If you don't differentiate your product or service, you are selling on price.
- All sales opportunities come from a customer's want or a need.
- When customers decide to buy they buy on value or price.
- Innovation can be successful in any market, not just technology.
- Your value proposition will drive branding, marketing, and sales.

See the workbook to develop your value proposition: http://www.bottomlinecoach.com/bd-workbook.

# Six

# Critical Paths

Face reality as it is, not as it was or as you wish
it to be.

—JACK WELCH

You've got a clear vision of where you want to be personally
and the timeframe in which you want that to become reality.
You have a target amount of money that you'll need to realize
that goal. You have a detailed analysis of where your organization
is now, both internally and externally in your market. You have a
well thought-out value proposition that you've discussed with key
customers, and they have agreed that it adds real value.

Now you're ready to prioritize the actions that must be added
to your business-development plan to move you forward on the
path to achieve your vision.

Critical paths are really goal categories, from each section of
your SWOT analysis. There should be no more than five to eight
top critical paths that you will focus on at a time. They should be

prioritized in order of having the biggest impact on growth and profitability as well as those representing the highest potential risk.

These critical paths should include all the functions in an organization and should ensure that the company can deliver what it sells, on time, at the highest quality, with value the customer recognizes. Everything else is secondary!

- What have you identified as your biggest weaknesses internally and biggest threats externally?
- Where are your best opportunities to maximize your strengths?
- What is the most important weakness to focus on?
- What has the most impact on the customer?
- How important is the weakness or threat to your business?
- What are the risks of not addressing the weakness or threat?
- What are the rewards of success?

When you have your critical goals documented, we'll use them as a road map to

- assign specific timed goals to your staff functions;
- drive delegation and accountability; and
- be the basis for regular progress reviews and updates as needed.

These will be discussed with your staff members, who will then assign specific actions to department and individual team members with measurements and clear expectations.

You're all done, right?

Not so fast. How will you measure the successful completion of each goal? If we are honest most of the critical things we identify to be fixed, and most of the best opportunities we've discovered aren't quick solutions. These will need to be accomplished over time with adjustments made as you learn more.

The best way to achieve goals is to develop agreed upon measurements and review trends of each of these measurements monthly. Use these metrics to create a dashboard to review on a regular basis. Review of these trends does several things:

- It tells people that the critical paths are important.
- It tells people you are committed to execution.
- It gives you the opportunity to ensure that the path is still valid, and to revise as necessary.

Most of the problems with strategy execution or change initiatives can be traced to this simple area: success isn't identified, measured, or rewarded. We try to hit vague, moving targets, people get frustrated and they give up.

Think about it. Over your career, how many quality, leadership, or other programs have you been associated with? How many of them produced results?

If you're like most of us, we've seen many programs and have seen few positive results. We will discuss this further in the section on execution and accountability.

## CHAPTER SUMMARY

- Use your SWOT analysis to prioritize critical paths. Address the largest potential for risk and the greatest opportunities first.

- Make sure you can deliver what you sell.
- Develop metrics, and trend results.
- Review progress monthly with all levels of the organization to show all stakeholders how and why they are important.

Go to your workbook and identify the top items to be worked as identified in your SWOT analysis: http://www.bottomlinecoach. com/bd-workbook.

# Section 3: Tactical Review and Plans

Seven

# Overview of the Business-Development Process

There are only two kinds of problems in business: growth problems and liquidation problems. Growth problems are better.

—Richard S. Sloma

A t this point, you have completed the following strategic tasks:

- Documented a clear vision.
- Generated a documented analysis of where you and your organization are currently.
- Prioritized the critical actions on your path.
- Developed a strong value proposition with which your customers agree.

You have the overall strategic path laid out to achieve your vision. This chapter begins the execution phase of the process.

In the following chapters, we will look at organizational functions and what is needed to execute the strategy outline we've developed.

Each function has a critical role in business development. No single function acting alone can provide long-term, sustainable, profitable growth. Larger companies and sadly even some smaller companies get caught in the "silo" trap. Each department has goals independent of the others, and some actually conflict with each other.

An example would be a health-care equipment manufacturer that I'm familiar with. They manufacture high-end equipment for home and hospital use. They are premium priced, and the equipment has numerous technical features. The sales organization is given increasingly higher sales quotas and year-over-year growth goals. The service department is given inventory goals that require spare parts inventory to be reduced year-over-year. So as the sales organization drives equipment population up, service management is driving the ability to support it down. Lack of support makes sales goals harder to accomplish, especially at a higher price points. While the problem seems obvious, the management teams of the two functions report through different paths at the corporate level and seemingly don't talk. So this problem continues year after year.

A synergistic approach to business development is critical.

Earlier I asked what business development means to you. For many it's just an updated term for sales or marketing, or both. We are all familiar with companies that have a business-development manager or executive. There are numerous ads looking for business-development managers, so, the term is well known. *However, this book is based on the understanding that the business-development executive is you, the top person in the company.*

My first book dealt with strategic planning. I talked about the reasons for business failure, and the common problem of most businesses not having documented plans. That's still as valid today is it was when I wrote that book. But strategy is only a single step of the solution. A tactical-execution plan is critical. As mentioned earlier, the real value in developing a plan is the planning process. But while the planning process helps you understand your business and markets better, regular review and execution is what builds tangible value in your organization. Robust execution of a good plan is better than weak execution of a perfect plan.

I've taken strategy a step further with the business-development process. I've built on developing a forward-looking strategy and added processes that build the foundation for sustained growth and earnings. I've also learned it's much more effective when tied to personal objectives because for business owners and C-level executives, that's what it comes down to. It's personal.

What do you think of when you hear the words "business-development"? If you think along the lines of sales, marketing, and partnerships, you are like most folks.

The best definition of business development I've seen (and one I happen to agree with) is from an article in *Forbes* by Scott Pollack[11]: "Business development is the creation of long-term value for an organization from customers, markets, and relationships."

---

11 Scott Pollack, "What, Exactly, Is Business Development?," *Forbes.com*, March 21, 2012, https://www.forbes.com/sites/scottpollack/2012/03/21/what-exactly-is-business-development/ - 2592b1a37fdb.

It isn't just about growth; it's about sustained growth, and building long-term value.

There have been numerous studies on business growth. From the high-growth gazelles studied by the SBA to David Thompson's book *Blueprint to a Billion*, they all say essentially the same thing. In his book, Thompson studied all companies that reached $1 billion in sales since going public after 1980. He found that all had at least five of the seven essentials that he details in his book.[12]

1. "Way-better" value to customers (a compelling value proposition)
2. High-growth market segment
3. Marquee customers
4. Big-brother alliances (partnering with large players in markets you want to enter)
5. Exponential returns
6. Inside-outside leadership
7. Board with essential experts (If you don't have a board, hire expert advisors.)

Now most of us are probably aren't interested in growing a billion-dollar company, but as you'll see in this book, many of these apply to midtier companies that want to develop sustainable growth and profits. The real focus is building long-term value. Sales and marketing can't do this alone. Partnerships with leading organizations or contracts with high-visibility customers just don't happen if your organization doesn't offer real value. So why aren't there more successful companies?

---

12 David G. Thomson, *Blueprint to a Billion* (John Wiley and Sons, 2006).

I may be a living example of the answer to that question. I left what was then a *Fortune* 500 company to start my own business. I left a secure, well-paying position, found investors, and founded a ground-up-start-up. I had no idea what I didn't know.

I was lucky I had started with a value proposition that was strong enough to overcome my lack of knowledge and inexperience. Our start-up grew to over six hundred employees in the United States and Europe, and about $50 million in sales.

Ten years later I left the company (as many founders do) and tried to decide what to do with the rest of my life. Responding to calls from a network of friends and connections, I began coaching businesses on strategy and business development, which I'm still doing sixteen years later. Those initial calls were often from banks, who were calling because loans were at risk. Turnarounds are frustrating and are usually "too little, too late." I began to develop a practice to help companies avoid the need for desperate measures.

So back to my original question. Why aren't there more successful companies?

I've spent the last thirty years working with companies from start-ups to midtier organizations in numerous markets and industries. The combination of my own business experience and what I've seen from the many others with whom I've worked with has provided me with a wealth of knowledge for which I'm grateful. I find that many business owners and CEOs are where I was way back then; they don't know what they don't know. Some recognize it and are open to learning and change, and some don't. Many spend very little time on strategy and immerse themselves in the day-to-day activities where they are all more comfortable seeing tangible results.

My experience has taught me that the talents and skills that got you into business are often not the ones that grow it, add shareholder value, and make it viable for the long term. My work over the past thirty years has taught me that business development is a process. It's not a department in the company; it isn't sales or marketing. It's an on-going learning and development process that never ends. What worked ten years ago isn't going to cut it today. The buying cycle has changed dramatically, and the buyer is more knowledgeable and has many options. That can be scary for business owners. It can also be a great opportunity. The playing field has changed, and small companies can compete more effectively with larger competitors if they know how.

There is so much more to developing a business that creates value for all stakeholders and customers than just sales or marketing. What good is a great sales team or an expensive marketing campaign do if you can't deliver on your commitments? Word of mouth and the Internet will make customer dissatisfaction more visible today than in the past. Quality, delivery, and customer perception of value, all generate unsolicited reviews, good or bad. True business development is a holistic approach to your business, delivering quality products or services that provide value to the customer, feeding an effective marketing strategy that drives sales. This approach makes marketing and sales more effective.

By now you should see that all facets of the organization must be in sync to build real value and repeatable profitable growth. The chart below is an overview of the process and we've covered the strategic part to this point.

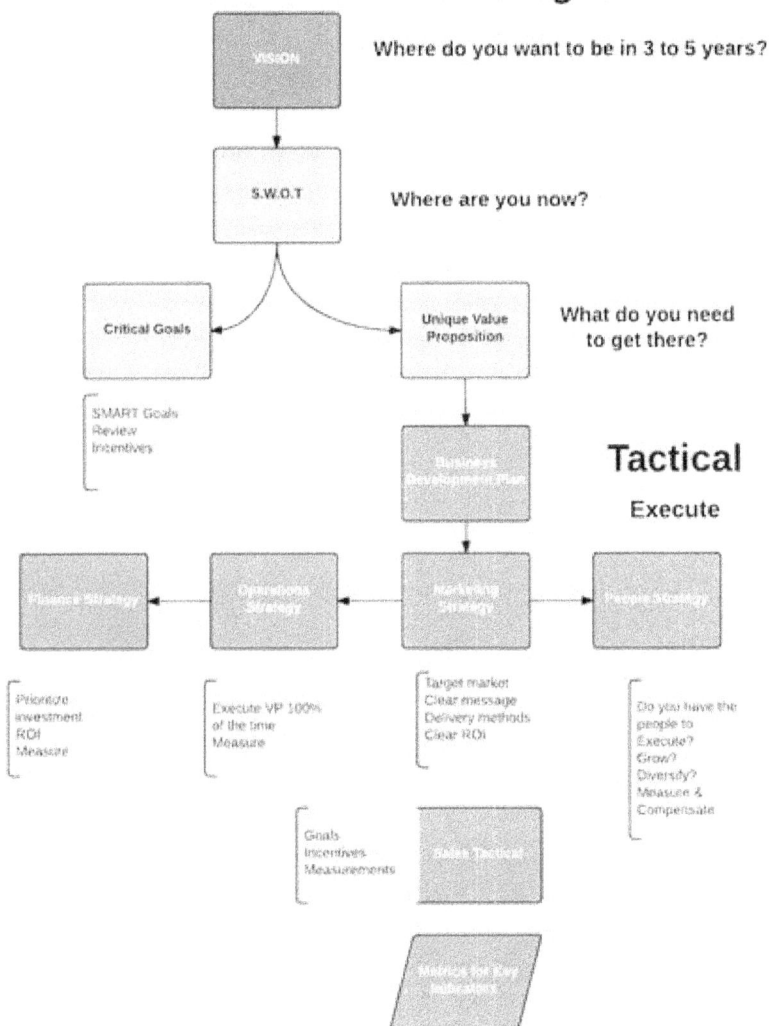

# Strategic

**Where do you want to be in 3 to 5 years?**

VISION

S.W.O.T

**Where are you now?**

Critical Goals

Unique Value Proposition

**What do you need to get there?**

SMART Goals
Review
Incentives

Business Development Plan

# Tactical

## Execute

Finance Strategy

Operations Strategy

Marketing Strategy

People Strategy

Prioritize
investment
ROI
Measure

Execute VP 100%
of the time
Measure

Target market
Clear message
Delivery methods
Clear ROI

Do you have the
people to
Execute?
Grow?
Diversify?
Measure &
Compensate

Goals
Incentives
Measurements

Sales Tactical

Metrics for Key
Indicators

## CHAPTER SUMMARY

- All organization functions are critical to business development that builds value.
- The business development in an organization is the CEO or owner.
- Business development is much more than sales or marketing.
- Business development is a process with trending measurements and regular review.

See the workbook at http://www.bottomlinecoach.com/bd-workbook.

Eight

# Barriers to Business Development

> Progress always involves risks. You can't steal
> second base and keep your foot on first.

> —FREDERICK WILCOX

You have embarked on a business-development process. Congratulations, you have now done more than about 50 percent of all businesses. According to various articles, the thinking is roughly 50 percent of all businesses don't have a documented business-development strategy. But before you pat yourself on the back, the tough part is just beginning.

According to Paul R. Niven, author of *Balanced Scorecard*, only 10 percent of those companies that have taken the trouble to document their plans execute them.[13] If those figures are correct, only 10 percent of 50 percent of all firms or about 5 percent overall have documented plans and executed them. It's interesting

---

13 Paul R. Niven, *Balanced Scorecard Step by Step* (John Wiley and Sons, 2006).

to note that various studies done by the SBA and others on fast-growth businesses say that only 4 percent of businesses are "gazelles," which is their term for fast-growth companies. The percentages seem to speak for themselves.

Planning creates negative responses from many business owners. I've heard many of them say that they completed a plan a few years back but nothing happened. When I dig into it, the real reason the plan failed is "nothing happened."

As stated many times in this book, a documented business plan by itself is of little value.

The value comes from the planning process. And the planning process isn't a "one and done" activity; it's an ongoing lifestyle change for you and your business.

According to Niven's work, the main reasons why only 10 percent execute their plans are as follows:

1. **Vision Barrier:** Only 5 percent of the workforce understands the strategy.
2. **People Barrier:** Only 25 percent of managers have incentives linked to strategy.
3. **Management Barrier:** 85 percent of executive teams spend less than one hour per month discussing strategy.
4. **Resource Barrier:** 60 percent of organizations don't link budgets to strategy.

Based on this, can any of us really question why most change initiatives fail?

I assume that Niven dealt with larger organizations, and I further assume that these numbers are probably conservative for smaller businesses. So, in addition to the communications and compensation problems listed above, what are the primary barriers to developing a business that creates value?

I wrote an e-book a few years back entitled "*11 Barriers to Business Development.*" I think it's important to understand these before we address the process. Some of them we've covered in previous chapters and some will come later.

1. Lack of direction (vision)
2. Lack of documented processes and infrastructure (You can't sell what you can't deliver.)
3. Poor strategic execution (focus on day-to-day)
4. Lack of employee engagement (excellent, motivated people in the right roles)
5. Leadership effectiveness
6. Access to cash or credit
7. Communications (internal and external)
8. Market intelligence
9. Marketing effectiveness
10. Lack of a compelling value proposition
11. Products or services that no longer meet market requirements

Items 4, 5, and 7 above deal with the main reason change initiatives fail: people! The title of this book, *Conscious Business Development*, says it all. If you as the leader of the organization don't *consciously* take steps every day to do the following, true sustainable long-term business development is unlikely.

- Communicate your strategy.
- Engage and motivate your people.
- Measure and review progress.
- Understand and remove obstacles.
- Hold people accountable starting with yourself.

The business-development process that follows, will address these barriers and more. It also includes a suggested schedule for plan review, accountability, and revision as needed.

We've addressed the strategic portion of your business-development plan, as well as your internal operations, and your external competition and markets. We will now move to the tactical portion of your business-development plan. That will include the following as a minimum:

- Defining your ideal buyer
- Deciding how you'll market and sell to those customers
- Planning your lead generation strategy
- Developing your marketing plan to generate leads
- Increase the effectiveness of your website and introducing inbound marketing
- Creating your tactical sales plan
- Developing your investment strategy
- Defining your people strategy
- Documenting your key performance indicators

## CHAPTER SUMMARY

- Many barriers to business development are internal.
- People are a critical link to value building, sustainable business development.

Go to the workbook and answer the evaluation questions on where you stand on these barriers currently: http://www.bottomlinecoach.com/bd-workbook.

Nine

# Treating the Symptoms

Change before you have to.

—JACK WELCH

One of the issues with executing a strategy for sustainable profitable growth is making excuses not to start. We think we are too busy with problems that arise, so we work on individual segments of the process, the current "hot spots." If you are spending excessive time putting out fires, that should alert you to the need to step back and understand the root causes.

It feels great to solve a problem; it's tangible, and we feel good about it. Executing a business-development strategy doesn't provide us with instant gratification. There are few immediate results. So it's easy to immerse ourselves into solving the problem of the day. Many who read this book are thinking, "I know I have to do this but I'm too busy now." My message is the same as the quote above; change is inevitable, so it's best to do it on your terms.

All too often we focus on the individual items that are causing us pain at the time. If we are experiencing flat or declining sales, we develop a new, short-term sales strategy; we lower prices, or come up with some type of special offer. We might even change sales management. But we often do that without spending the time to understand why sales are declining, and what is the best way to solve the problem and keep it from reoccurring. If we wait too long to address problems, we begin to reduce our options of how to address them.

Use the five why's as a process to get to root cause. Here is a simplified example:

| | |
|---|---|
| Problem. Sales are declining | Why? |
| Key customer has moved to a competitor | Why? |
| Competitor has a new product that outperforms ours | Why? |
| We reduced investment in R & D | Why? |
| We decided to defend and extend our existing product | Why? |
| To generate short-term profits and maximize bonuses | Root |

Now we have reduced our options. Change will likely not occur on our terms. Actually, the example above happened at a company with which I was familiar. If the company had a review process, it's leaders might have made better decisions.

The image below represents what should happen when you become aware of a need to change.

When a symptom such as reduced margins or declining sales comes to your attention, it's time to step back and understand why. If you are trending key performance indicators, you can see when the problem began. Put a team together to understand the root cause of the issue. If it requires significant change, the first step is awareness of a need to change. That awareness must be followed by planning and commitment.

**Problems or symptoms**

Declining profit
Flat sales growth
Declining market share
Poor lead generation
Inability to manage change

**Drives awareness and need to change**

↓

**Should lead to ...**
**Corporate strategy**

Vision
SWOT
UVP

Drives ↗

**Marketing Strategy**

Brand
Position in the market
Value proposition

↓Drives

**Sales strategy**
How you sell
Understand what benefits you provide or what problems you solve
Sell on value not price alone

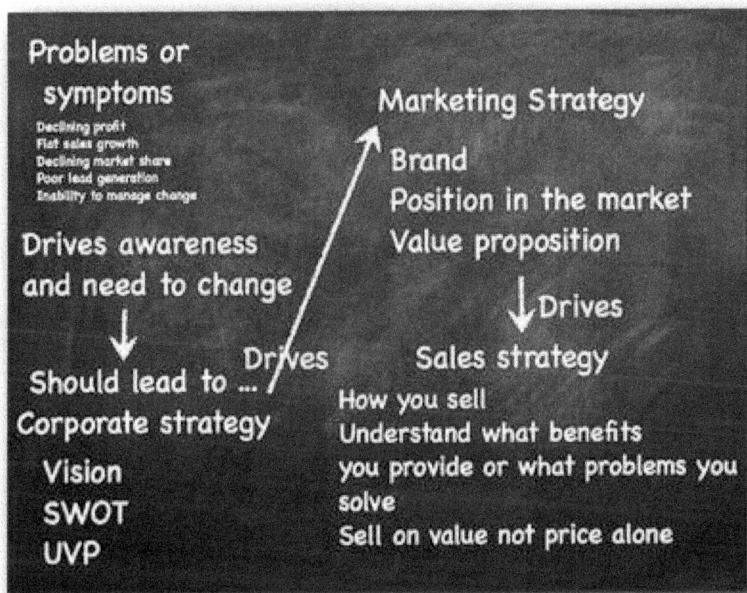

Review your business plan, and understand what's still relevant and what needs to be updated. If you are doing this on a regular basis, you will already have seen the trend and have begun working on a solution.

The key is to *consciously* work to be proactive and stop treating symptoms. When we lose a customer, and experience a revenue drop, the instinct is to light a fire under sales to go find a new one. Leadership isn't about fixing problems quickly and efficiently; it's about preventing them in the first place.

A high percentage of the time events that happen are symptoms of larger problems below the surface. Solving the immediate problem, without addressing the root cause, is treating the symptom. Taking a few hours, each month for you and your staff to develop a planning and review process isn't a nicety, it's critical.

It is not necessary to change. Survival is not mandatory.

—W. Edwards Deming

Putting off developing a planning and review process is dangerous because no matter what business you're in, change will impact you. You, as the CEO or owner, must *consciously* decide to document your sustainable business-development strategy, and execute it. It's not enough to develop a plan with the top-management team and delegate execution down the chain. You must make a *conscious* effort to be engaged, and aware of progress and trends. If it isn't important to you, it certainly won't be to anyone else.

Using the critical paths identified in chapter 6, do an in-depth root-cause analysis to determine what caused the issue, and eliminate problems and barriers to growth. Taking the time to understand the root cause will make developing a better solution easier.

Also, look at the barriers to growth in chapter 8. (They are also listed in the workbook.) How many of these are present in your organization? Put a team together with representative from each major function, and do a root-cause analysis to understand and begin to eliminate the barriers. Again, you must be willing to listen and be open to discussion to convey the message that you are serious and are behind the process.

Before you begin execution of your business-development strategy, you need to understand and remove these barriers.

## CHAPTER SUMMARY

- Leadership isn't about fixing problems quickly and efficiently; it's about preventing them in the first place.
- Barriers to growth and business development exist in all organizations.
- It's not enough to treat the symptoms. You must identify and eliminate the root cause.
- Change is inevitable. Change before you have to, and change on your own terms.

See the workbook for questions on this chapter: http://www.bottomlinecoach.com/bd-workbook.

Ten

# Marketing and Sales

Content marketing is the only marketing left.

—Seth Godin

S uccessful companies realize there are clearly defined roles for both.

A definition of marketing I found in a dictionary is "the action or business of promoting and selling products or services, including market research and advertising."

Even that definition confuses the role with sales.

A better definition from The American Marketing Association says, "Marketing is the activity, set of institutions, and processes for creating, communicating, delivering, and exchanging offerings that have value for customers, clients, partners, and society at large."[14]

I like to think of marketing as an educational process with which you help the customers understand the benefits they

---

14 "American Marketing Association Approved July 2013," https://www.ama.org/AboutAMA/Pages/Definition-of-Marketing.aspx.

receive from your product or service and help them to understand the true value. When it comes down to selling anything, *price and value are all that matters.* If your marketing doesn't help the customer understand the value of your product, all that's left is price. *Price is determined by what the customer will pay for the value perceived.*

Many companies price products by some percentage over product cost. That may be the price you need to make a profit, but it may not be what the customer is willing to pay. *There is no purchase where price exceeds perceived value.*

From a customer prospective, perceived value is the benefits received from the product minus the cost they paid for it.

In chapter 5 we discussed a unique value proposition and learned that this would be the basis for our marketing and sales plans. So we can begin to see that marketing plays a critical role in positioning your product or service in the market and receiving the best possible price for it. It's more critical than ever in today's environment to have a clean, compelling marketing message. Potential customers are overwhelmed with e-mails, cold calls, direct mail, and advertising. These methods simply don't work as well as they did even ten years ago.

By "marketing message," I don't mean creating a catchy slogan or clever logo. I mean a clear message to your target buyer that spells out the benefits they will gain from your product or service. A clear marketing message starts with your unique value proposition.

A clear marketing message must

- be aimed directly at your ideal buyer;
- be communicated in terms that the buyers use and understand;

- present a clear definition of their problems and your understanding of them;
- present your solutions to those problems; and
- show why you do it better, and faster, and deliver more value than your competition.

You must ensure that your prospective customer knows about your product, and more importantly understands how it will benefit him or her. Sales alone won't do it. When I talk to a salesperson my radar is up. Even if that is knowledgeable about the product and seems sincere, I know that his or her job is to sell me something.

According to an article in *Adweek*, 81 percent of shoppers conduct online research before buying. And 78 percent of local mobile searches result in off-line purchases.[15]

I can't think of a single significant thing that I've purchased in the past few years that I haven't researched online, by comparing reviews.

Yet, according to a survey by Score, about half of small businesses don't even have websites, and 91 percent of them aren't mobile optimized.[16] Midsize companies have a higher percentage of businesses with websites, but they are often used as a static catalog. There are over one billion websites on the web today, so even if you have one, what are the chances of yours being found

15 Kimberly Morrison, "81% of Shoppers Conduct Online Research Before Buying," November 28, 2014, http://www.adweek.com/digital/81-shoppers-conduct-online-research-making-purchase-infographic/.

16 Rieva Lesonsky, "It's 2017. How Can You Not Have a Website Yet?" January 3, 2017, https://www.score.org/blog/its-2017-how-can-you-not-have-website-yet.

in a search? The quote at the beginning of this chapter says it all: "Content marketing is the only marketing left."

Content marketing is the creation and sharing of valuable information online that positions you as the subject-matter expert on your product or service. Many companies have blogs. They post things that are interesting to them: news updates or financial-news updates. The issue with this is that for the most part, nobody is interested in the things that interest you. Potential customers are interested in their problems or opportunities and in the best options to meet those challenges or opportunities.

## THE BUYER'S JOURNEY
All buyers making significant purchases that impact their businesses follow the same basic path.

- **Awareness stage:** They look for information verifying that they indeed have a problem or opportunity. Is there more information on it from independent sources?
- **Consideration stage:** The prospect has clearly defined the problem or opportunity and is researching all the available approaches, methods, or products that solves their problem.
- **Decision stage:** The prospect has decided which solution he or she wants and begins searching for vendors and products. Prospects read reviews, and compare benefits, and pricing.

Blogging is a great way to communicate your expertise in the problem or opportunity and why your company is the best one to address it. Frequent blogging also provides an excellent platform for search-engine optimization. Companies that offer SEO services to maximize your website's visibility are addressing a single point in time. Doing it once provides little actual value over the long term. Google looks for fresh content in its algorithms.

Each blog post is a web page and an opportunity to reach your buyer. When a blog post is published, it stays in the search results indefinitely. Some of my most-read blog posts were published several years ago. Each post presents an opportunity to be found in a search, and have someone visit your website.

What are the customers in your market concerned about? If you are regularly publishing blog posts that provide current and valuable information on what interests them, they will find you.

Content marketing is permission-based marketing compared to traditional interruption marketing. If a customer searches for information, and lands on your site, fills out a form giving you contact information in exchange for a valuable offer such as a white paper or e-book with great information on the subject in which he or she is interested, they have become a qualified lead. If you aren't getting people to your website by supplying valuable information, you're going to be left behind.

The business process discussed in this book focuses on marketing as an education tool and on sales as a facilitation tool. The role of marketing is to help customers better understand their needs and why your product or service provides the best solution to those needs. The primary role of sales is to facilitate the sales process and make it a positive customer experience.

The first step in marketing is understanding who exactly is your ideal buyer. One of my clients is a manufacturer of products for oil and gas as well as the automotive industry.

Historically, this client's primary buyers were the purchasing managers at their customers' companies. After going through our process, we determined that the purchasing managers were only interested in two things: price and delivery. My client's management didn't differentiate the company on either of these. We decided the client's ideal buyers were the people in the engineering or R&D functions who recognized the value that the client was able to provide over the competition. The technical function would then notify purchasing that this was the product that was needed. The buying determination became based on value and not price. This strategy has proven very successful and led to some major opportunities in the client's markets. Their company's market is global, and the client has replaced direct sales with inbound marketing as the primary lead generator.

So content marketing, or inbound marketing, is simply providing enough valuable and useful information, to your ideal buyers, to allow them to find you. Inbound marketing is permission based and not interruption based, like traditional marketing. This is different than advertising, where you broadcast your message to everyone and get little return on your investment. With permission-based marketing, you get fewer leads but they are better leads because they are coming from your ideal buyer. Best of all, it's cost-effective, you invest time, not money as your primary resource.

When you turn leads over to sales, they are qualified leads, and using contact-management software (CRM), you are knowledgeable about what the prospects are interested in by the pages they visited, and the downloads they requested.

## CHAPTER SUMMARY

- Marketing and sales have distinct roles.
- When selling anything, price and value are all that matters.
- There is no purchase when price exceeds perceived value.
- Marketing educates your customer of the benefits and value they receive from your product or service.
- Traditional, interruption-based marketing is becoming less effective.
- Content and web-based marketing costs less and more effective in getting your message out.
- Your website cannot not be static if you want people to find you.
- Eighty-one percent of buyers conduct online research before buying.
- Blogging is an effective lead generation tool.

See the workbook to evaluate your marketing and sales operations: http://www.bottomlinecoach.com/bd-workbook.

Eleven

# Operations

There is nothing so useless as doing efficiently
that which should not be done at all.

—Peter F. Drucker

Your business-development strategy must include operations. No matter how clear your message is, and how well you market it, it's all for nothing if you can't deliver a quality product or service on time, at a profit, all the time. In many companies, such as in manufacturing organizations, operations are a cost center, and include most of the labor costs. In service businesses, it's a revenue generator. But it's often treated as an afterthought in strategic planning, even though if operations aren't successful, nothing else can be.

As mentioned in an earlier example, I've seen many companies at which operations and sales report to different executives with different incentives. The sales and marketing teams are driven to grow sales, and the operations teams are tasked with reducing costs. "Do more with less" is rarely an effective growth strategy. In most cases that drives a customer-satisfaction problem.

A great example of this problem is another health-care company with which I'm familiar. The sales department is tasked with growing their regional markets 6–10 percent per year. Operations management (in this case, home-care nurses and administrators) is measured on profit and costs. The two divisions report up through different chains and have little, if any, cross-leadership. The operations functions are incentivized on cost savings and are reluctant to invest in training on new services. Sales is tasked with trying to sell new services that aren't being provided. In this scenario who is managing the customer? If you answered "nobody," you're correct. How much time do you spend aligning goals and incentive plans to support your strategy?

Another example was my own company. I founded a value-added logistics company in Memphis Tennessee. Memphis is the home of FedEx and is marketed as the distribution center of America. My customers were computer manufactures for the most part, and we worked with them to outsource some or all of their logistics services to us.

We worked with them to understand their then-current processes to build a cost model for a proposal. In almost every case, especially in the larger companies, we found conflicting goals as some of the main drivers of costs. A typical analysis would surprise the prospect and would look something like this:

- The inventory manager was tasked with managing inventory. This is critical in high-tech companies since products and parts become obsolete so quickly. Inventory levels were a key performance indicator and watched carefully.

- The repair center managers were tasked with getting product refurbished at the lowest cost possible. They found that they could do that if they held material until they got minimum quantities to get discounts. Repair costs were not a KPIs, and the repair managers were usually not in the inventory reporting chains.
- The freight management was measured on freight costs. Again, someone was holding material to get a full truckload that saved freight dollars. Freight costs were looked at in total, and not broken out by function.

This was a great opportunity for root-cause analysis, which is what we did. All of this batching was driving up inventory levels steadily. We offered pipeline management and averaged a seven-day turn as opposed to months in some cases. Inventory reduction and increased customer satisfaction were what we competed on and were evaluated on.

The message here is that all were large companies with brand recognition. Their core business was developing the newest and greatest computer and marketing it. Most didn't include logistics and distribution as critical paths in their strategies.

What crucial role will your operation functions play in achieving your vision? How will you measure performance to ensure quality at a profit? How will you incentivize the function to support other functions?

## WHAT SHOULD YOU STOP DOING?

One of the ways to make operations more efficient is to stop doing unnecessary things. That may sound like an obvious statement, but the mind-set of "We've always done it that way" is alive and well. Look at your operations as an outsider, and look for wasted efforts:

- Reports that nobody uses
- Repetitive tasks
- Jobs overlapping
- Wasted steps in processes that are no longer needed

Every company is doing something that no longer needs to be done. To an outsider with no knowledge of how things got started, many of these are fairly obvious. I know from my own experience that it's tough to look at your operations as an outsider.

Part of your annual operations plan should include value-stream mapping to streamline processes.

## IF IT IMPACTS THE CUSTOMER OR PROFITABILITY MEASURE IT!

What's important for you to look at and review with your management team?

Maybe a better way to ask that question is how many of the following do you see?

- Missed ship dates
- Excessive overtime
- High employee turnover
- High level of customer returns
- Excessive waste
- High level of downtime
- Low level of inventory turns

All of these have direct impacts on customer satisfaction and profitability. Are you trending your key indicators? Many companies I see measure some of these things, but they look at them as snapshots on a monthly basis. To be meaningful you have to establish a baseline and look at trends.

You also have to review these with operations management on a regular basis, and expect plans for any metrics that are trending the wrong way. As a leader, you must drive accountability to the people making the product or delivering the service.

## COMMUNICATIONS

As is evidenced by the examples above communications across functions is critical, not only at the management level but also at the point at which the work is being done. While this may seem like an obvious statement, it's one of the most common issues I see when I'm exposed to a company. This happens in small companies as well as large organizations. Silos are deadly in any size of an organization.

Do your operations people understand your business-development strategy, your value proposition, and their roles in it? Having an understanding of the parts they play in the overall strategy leads to suggestions, engagement, and higher productivity. Attracting and retaining excellent people should be a critical part of your operations plan. Involving them in the overall vision of the company provides job enrichment and engagement. Help them to understand that when they produce their widgets, they are actually helping to produce a car, or an airplane. Post pictures of the final product your product is used in, and help employees understand the importance of what they do.

## OPERATIONS ROLE IN SALES

We all agree that service personnel play a key role on sales. They are the face of the company when they interact with your customer. Manufacturing employees also have a critical role in customer perception. I have done dozens of plant tours. During those tours, I form an opinion of the company within the first five or ten minutes. What I hear from the executive staff must be carried forward to the plant floor.

I came across a report done by IQMS, a company that sells ERP software. IQMS had a table in their report listing what manufacturers say customers look for during site visits.[17] The information in the report closely mirrored what I look for when I visit a plant.

- Sixty-one percent look for a commitment to quality and continuous improvement.
- Fifty-two percent look for professional, clean, and efficient operations.
- Fifty percent look for unique technical and professional skills.
- Twenty-four percent look at capacity and plant equipment.
- Seventeen percent look at the skill of the workforce.

The impression of your operations functions, gained by your customer or prospective customer during a site visit, can complement or destroy your sales and marketing message.

---

17 Creating Sustainable Business Report, http://learn.mbtmag.com/creating-sustainable-business-growth?abm_pos=2&abm_adtype=whitepaper_ad&abm_type=image&abm_adcategory=lead_gen_item.

## CHAPTER SUMMARY

- Value-driven sustainable business development is only possible when you deliver a quality product, on-time, at a profit, every time.
- Your operations goals must be aligned with all other functions in your organization, and they must understand why their role is important.
- Develop key performance indicators that are critical to your success, and trend them on a rolling twelve-month cycle.
- Make sure all functions of KPIs are aligned.
- Involve operations people in the big picture to sustain engagement.
- Everybody has a role in sales and customer retention.

See the workbook at http://www.bottomlinecoach.com/bd-workbook.

# Twelve

# People

If you don't understand people, you don't
understand business.

—Simon Sinek

As I write this book, there's a lot of talk about bringing good paying jobs back to America. That's an admirable goal, but there's another side to it.

In my humble opinion, finding and hiring qualified people is the biggest problem for business today. I know several of my clients are limiting growth specifically for that reason. They are turning away business because they can't get a reliable workforce in increasing numbers!

In my first book, I wrote about the impact on the organization of leaving underperformers in their jobs. Allowing poor performance to continue can impact everyone. I also cautioned management from organizing around people's abilities. Structure the organization in a way that best serves the customer, and provides the best return on investment. Then evaluate your staff, and put the best-qualified person in each slot, rather than trying to organize around good and subpar performance. Today's environment is causing business owners and CEO's to be reluctant to make changes. The old "devil you know versus the devil you don't know" scenario is prevalent.

People are either viewed as costs or investments. How important they are to you and your business indicates one or the other. Earlier we discussed the lack of employee engagement that exists today. We all agree that employees have little or no loyalty to companies anymore. But what about loyalty to employees?

Business has caused some of today's issues. I had a discussion with a client a while back, and he made an interesting point. Somewhere in the 1980s, companies started seeing people as "head count" as in "We have to reduce head count." I'm not talking strictly about unskilled labor; I include technical and administrative people as well.

The use of temporary, or contract labor, became common to better manage labor costs during peak and slow times. In addition, hiring part-time employees (nine under thirty hours per week) to reduce benefits expenses became more acceptable. This has morphed into a low-skilled workforce that accepts employment through temp agencies as a way of life. They have little expectations of full-time work and being able to grow with a company, moving on has become common for them.

Large corporations outsourcing manufacturing jobs offshore for lower labor costs, or instituting layoffs to keep a stock price up have certainly contributed to this problem.

The government also has contributed in several ways.

- The historical high corporate-tax rate has driven investment offshore and has reduced skilled jobs, and thereby skilled workers, through lack of apprenticeships.

- The welfare benefits and entitlements are to blame as well. Michael Tanner published an article in the *National Review*, on August 21, 2013, about a study done by the Cato Institute. That article entitled "Welfare: A Better Deal than Work" states that there are 126 separate federal programs for low-income individuals,[18] in addition to state programs. The Cato study also states that median value of the welfare package across the fifty states is about $28,800. Broken down at an hourly rate (forty hours per week), it's about $13.70 per hour. But health care is included in that number, so a person working for you with a family would need to pick up some or all of their health-care costs. In addition, the IRS states that welfare payments are exempt from taxation. That means you would need to pay a person about $20.00 per hour based on the average to make working be a better deal. Many employers would be hard pressed to pay $20 per hour for unskilled labor.

Before I upset anyone, I'm not saying that I'm for, or against the programs; I'm simply stating facts on the difficulty of finding and keeping employees in the current environment. True, $28,800 doesn't provide a great standard of living, but the folks on the production floor making $13.70 per hour or even $15.00 per hour are actually worse off. The article refers to surveys that say many of these people would prefer to be working and that they just can't afford the reduction of income.

---

18 Michael Tanner, "Welfare: A Better Deal than Work," August 21, 2013, http://www.nationalreview.com/article/356317/welfare-better-deal-work-michael-tanner.

That's one set of issues. Another has to do with the expectations of younger people. A Generation Y (twenty-two- to twenty-nine-year-olds) workplace expectations study by American Express and Gen Y Research,[19] which received survey responses from one thousand managers, finds some interesting statistics:

- Gen Y employees have unrealistic compensation expectations (51 percent).
- These employees are perceived to have a poor work ethic (47 percent).
- These employees are easily distracted (46 percent).
- Generation Y employees have an overall positive view of management, believing they can provide experience (59 percent) and wisdom (41 percent).

Some say they also lack certain interpersonal skills, because of the level of interaction with technology and the reduction of face time.

There is clearly a gap between management expectations of Generation Y employees and their perception of work overall.

So those are the facts. Now what do you do about them? You still need quality people if you are going to grow your business. How will you do that?

Well, clearly, you have to find a way to pay a living wage, but there has to be more to it than that. As employers, we need to rethink our relationships with the workforce. The world has moved from the agricultural age, to the industrial age, and now to the information age. However, most of our thinking and management techniques are still in the industrial age. Management sets the

---

19 "American Express Gen Y Workplace Study," http://millennialbranding. com/american-express-study/.

strategy and delegates actions, and the bulk of the workforce doesn't have a need to know. Then we wonder why we don't have buy in to our plans.

The problems above were over thirty years in the making and are not going to be solved on a macro scale. No one is going to sign a paper and make it all go away.

There are several steps that each owner or CEO must take in order to develop people:

1. We have to take a hard look at who's employed now. What strengths can we build on, and what weaknesses can we correct through coaching? Are they in the right positions today?
2. We have to develop a retention policy to keep good people working with us.
3. We have to develop a reputation in the market place that we are the best company to work for to attract good people. (Blogging helps here as well.)
4. We have to be creative in our incentive and compensation policies to not just deliver dollars but also participation and recognition.

I understand you can't instantly give everyone big raises and I don't think those will be the solution anyway. One client I have has a large number of low-skill-level employees. New hires make about $12.00 to $13.00 per hour. But he has incentive programs that allow an employee to make between $45,000 and $50,000 per year. He's done a great job designing incentives that allow him to get good returns on the extra money invested, while retaining experienced employees.

He also makes the environment fun with various gatherings and recognition events. As a result, his turnover for who remain on the job over six months is near zero. His customer retention rate is near 100 percent, so his employees are clearly buying in to his strategy. He sees people as investments, does a lot of coaching, and develops processes and training to make sure they understand the job and their role. He also meets with both shifts of employees every day. He has made a decision to *consciously* create his own workforce. It can be done, but we have to get creative.

## CHAPTER SUMMARY

- Finding and retaining quality labor is going to take creative incentives and *conscious* job enrichment.
- People were viewed as a cost in industrial-age-thinking organizations; we must consider them an investment in the information age.
- Like it or not, we are competing with government programs with salary and benefits. We need to get creative.
- Social media can be a great tool for attracting people and explaining benefits of working with your company. It can spread negative views about your company as well.
- Generation Y employees will take some additional coaching and support.
- We have to consciously improve job enrichment in all levels of the organization.

See the workbook at http://www.bottomlinecoach.com/bd-workbook.

Thirteen

# Finance

If you would know the value of money, go and try
to borrow some.

—Benjamin Franklin

I think we all agree that developing growth strategies without
access to cash or credit to execute makes the attainment of
your goals a dream. When we follow all the steps in this book and
have a well-thought-out and documented business-development
plan, a portion of the financial assets of the company must be
allocated to implementation.

The purposes of the planning process as it relates to finance
as a minimum are to:

- Look for and eliminate internal issues with cash. Waste
  and overtime related to rework, scrap, and slow-moving
  inventory are all expenditures that could be allocated to
  new products or services.
- Understand what the company needs to do, and put a
  financial forecast together that shows estimated financial

needs as well as return on investment. This forecast must include capital expenditures as well as labor resources needed to execute strategic initiatives.

- Provide the information to prioritize spending between operations as they exist today and growth.
- Develop key-metrics trends that you can use to explain to a potential lender that you have a plan and are executing it.

Whether you need to borrow money to implement or not, all of this must be considered. If you don't invest for implementation, you won't execute. Government loans such as SBA (or USDA for rural settings) are only guarantees to the lender. That means that a bank has to approve your request and then submit a package to a guarantor seeking its approval.

Banks are in the loan business, not in the risk business. They will not work off lofty forecasts. They look at how your company is operating now, and how you've operated historically. They use that information before they ever consider forecasts. Banks or private investors will all want the same things: a documented plan showing historical performance, and a well-thought-out business-development plan with the following items as a minimum:

- Three- to five-year historical financials
- Three- to five-year forecasts
- Cash flows and balance sheets
- A market analysis relative to demographics, competitors, etc.
- A document showing that your growth plan has a tactical portion to make investors comfortable that you know what you're doing

Many companies I've been involved with have great ideas, and when the need for financing comes up, we start from scratch by creating a miniprospectus. As I said in earlier chapters, you should always have your company ready to sell. Add this: you should always have your company in a position to attract credit or equity investment to take advantage of opportunities. Having a prospectus on file to be updated as part of your annual business-development plan review keeps the focus on what you're trying to do, and it can save weeks of hectic work should investment be required.

By now, I hope you are beginning to understand that sustainable business development isn't a department. It's the entire company starting with you.

## CHAPTER SUMMARY

- Business-development strategies must be funded as well as current operations.
- Document the financial strategy in a prospectus and keep in on file to be updated annually.

Look at the questions related to finance in your workbook: http://www.bottomlinecoach.com/bd-workbook.

# Section 4: Execution and Accountability

Fourteen

# Organizational Culture

The world as we have created it is a process
of our thinking. It cannot be changed without
changing our thinking.

—Albert Einstein

The business-development process documented here can
help you see areas of your company more clearly. It will also
help you evaluate management-team members and generate
ideas for new products and services. But developing the plan
is useless unless you make a *conscious* effort and commitment
to change. Take a hard look at your management team and the
organization's culture. Are you in the best position to move forward with sustainable business development? How many of these
issues are currently present in your organization?

- Excessive meetings with no agenda and no results
- Consensus-driven decision making
- Lack of personal accountability

- Poor communication between entities
- Reluctance to terminate poor performers
- Misaligned and uncoordinated efforts (silo effect)
- Personality conflicts and power struggles
- Apathetic and unmotivated employees
- Inconsistent results
- Poor time management
- Reactive rather than proactive effort
- Micromanagement
- Declining sales or market share
- Lack of teamwork
- Duplication of effort
- High employee turnover
- Substandard quality
- Numerous unresolved issues and postponed decisions

We've covered some of these in earlier chapters, but as you can see, many deal with management behavior and how you and your staff function as a team. Has your vision for the company been explained to all stakeholders? Has it been done accurately? Remember information from and to the CEO is filtered by layers. The message here is that cultural change starts with you and moves to your staff and to all stakeholders. If you aren't accountable or seen as a part of a cohesive team, how can you expect excellent results?

There are hundreds of quotes on culture. A Google search gave me 29,400,000 results!

But the issues above dictate your culture more clearly than any quote. What are the issues above telling us?

- Lack of leadership
- Poor communication
- Fear of failure (warranted or not)
- Lack of direction
- Numerous additional examples (you get the idea)

You need to look at your management team and honestly decide which of the above are holding you back. Remember the employee-engagement statistics we reviewed earlier. The issues listed above are all part of the lack of employee engagement.

An article in *Inc.* online gave the top seven reasons the best employees quit their jobs[20]:

1. Stagnation (it's hard to offer advancement if the company isn't growing.)
2. Overwork (could this be the result of relying on too few employees while keeping underperformers?)
3. Poor vision and transition to firm goals (execution)
4. Lack of respect for people (profit over people)
5. Lack of recognition
6. Lack of trust
7. Excessive hierarchy

Developing a culture of recognition and respect is critical with today's workforce. If you aren't willing to make a *conscious* effort

---

20 Lolly Daskal, "7 Reasons the Best Employees Quit, Even When They Like Their Job," https://www.inc.com/lolly-daskal/7-reasons-the-best-employees-quit-even-when-they-like-their-job.html.

to address the issues above, you will not develop a culture that attracts and retains excellent people.

## CHAPTER SUMMARY

- Retaining great people and customers requires a great culture. If your employees are engaged, that will be obvious to your customers.
- Culture is determined by leadership starting with you.

Look at the workbook to evaluate your culture today: http://www. bottomlinecoach.com/bd-workbook.

Fifteen

# Review, Rethink, and Respond with Conscious Action

Plans are nothing, planning is everything.

—Philip Kotler

I've seen many business owners and CEOs over the years making the effort to develop a plan, or change initiatives and then delegate implementation of the plan down to staff. They often don't give it another thought. The business-development process outlined in this book, and the accompanying workbook is not a one-and-done activity. The process is never done. It requires review, revision as market demands change, and *conscious* commitment to action.

We've all heard this old saying: How do you eat an elephant? One bite at a time.

Sustainable business development is an elephant. As you can see from this book, there are lots of moving parts. They have to be broken down into short-term actions and goals and reviewed at the top-management level on a regular basis.

- Are the goals assigned to the critical paths moving forward?
- If not, why not?
- What has changed that makes this task a higher or lower priority?
- What opportunities or issues have arisen since the plan was completed?
- Is there accountability at all levels?
- What are our key performance indicators telling us? Are we improving?
- Are we getting returns on the investments we've made?

All of this sounds like common sense. And it is! But it rarely gets done. It takes a *conscious* effort on the part of the owner or CEO to be accountable to execution if you expect anyone else to be.

When I work with clients, I suggest that goals should be reviewed and discussed on a monthly basis, with in-depth reviews each quarter. The entire planning process should be reviewed annually for currency and revised as needed. As I said in the beginning, it's not a plan, it's a process.

If you think that's a big commitment, you are correct. But it's better than meeting trying to figure out how to save your business because something came up that you should have seen and prepared for.

## CHAPTER SUMMARY

- Repeatable business development is an on-going process.
- Regularly scheduled reviews are required at all levels to understand issues and changes and to keep them in everyone's focus.

Sixteen

# Commitment

The definition of insanity is "Doing what you
have always done and expecting a different
result."

—ALBERT EINSTEIN

We covered the statistics in a previous chapter stating us
that only 10 percent of companies effectively execute their
strategies and change initiatives. It seems that once they have a
plan, they convince themselves the work is done. The value isn't
in the plan document; that's just a placeholder. The value comes
from the planning process and from fearless execution.

It takes an unrelenting and visible commitment of the business owner or CEO to execute effectively. The hard part of strategy execution is that it's a long-term effort. We are living in a
world of instant gratification; we aren't happy when things take
time. Great companies that produce sustainable growth and profits aren't lucky they understand their internal issues and where the
market is going. They change before they have to.

You must approach every day with a *conscious* commitment to create value in your organization and in your people.

- You must have regular monthly reviews with the managers of all departments together. Dialogue is critical to execution.
- Be relentless in asking questions and removing obstacles.
- Quarterly reviews should take quick looks at your assumptions to see if revision is needed.
- An annual review should be a review of the entire plan for currency and market acceptance or changes.

I use a relatively inexpensive, cloud-based project-management software with my clients to track actions and updates. The one I use is Wrike, because it's fairly robust and very easy to use. This makes sure all stakeholders know what's going on relative to execution.

If you aren't committed to change, you can bet that no one else will be.

## CHAPTER SUMMARY

- Hold monthly reviews with all major departments to understand interactions (no silos).
- *Consciously* commit to review and execute.
- Be accountable and hold others accountable.

See the workbook at http://www.bottomlinecoach.com/bd-workbook.

# About the Author

Martin Harshberger, the founder and president of Measurable Results LLC and BottomLineCoach.com, is a management consultant and business coach. During a successful career spanning more than thirty-five years, he has held executive positions with, and consulted for a broad range of businesses, from start-ups to *Fortune* 500 companies.

From 1979 to 1989, Mr. Harshberger held senior-executive positions with international responsibilities in operations and manufacturing at Control Data Corporation, which at the time was one of the world's leading manufacturers of mainframe computers.

In 1989, Martin founded Logistics Management Inc. (LMI), a pioneer in the field of value-added logistics management. Serving as its CEO, he led this Memphis-based company from the startup phase to nearly $50 million in sales within ten years. *Inc.* magazine named LMI one of America's five hundred fastest-growing companies.

After selling his share of LMI in 1999, Martin served as CEO of a midsize manufacturing company in the HVAC industry for five years. In 2005, he founded Measurable Results LLC.

Mr. Harshberger is passionate about helping companies grow and prosper in today's rapidly changing global economy. His results-oriented, no-fads, no-frills approach is especially helpful to companies that want to differentiate and create value.

He believes that success in today's environment will require *conscious* thought and a commitment to execution.

Martin lives in northeastern Mississippi with his wife, Marla, and faithful executive assistant (dog), Sadie.

# About the Company

Measurable Results LLC was founded in 2005 primarily as a turnaround consulting firm. We have modified our offerings over the past thirteen years to try to eliminate the causes of the need for turnarounds. We focus on helping seven- and eight-figure manufacturing, distribution, and select service companies build repeatable, sustainable value through our business-development process.

# Contact Information

Martin can be contacted at his website, http://www.bottomline-coach.com/contact-us

or e-mail at martin@bottomlinecoach.com.

# Bibliography

Altman, Jack. "Don't Be Surprised When Your Employees Quit." *Forbes*, February 22, 2017, 25. https://www.forbes.com/sites/valleyvoices/2017/02/22/dont-be-surprised-when-your-employees-quit/ - 4b7d40ba325e.

"American Express Gen Y Workplace Study." 84. http://millennial-branding.com/american-express-study/.

"American Marketing Association Approved July 2013." 70. https://www.ama.org/AboutAMA/Pages/Definition-of-Marketing.aspx.

Attard, Janet. "How Much Do Small Businesses Really Earn?" January 9, 2017, 15. https://www.businessknowhow.com/money/earn.htm.

"Creating Sustainable Business Report." 80. http://learn.mbt-mag.com/creating-sustainable-business-growth?abm_pos=2&abm_adtype=whitepaper_ad&abm_type=image&abm_adcategory=lead_gen_item.

Crum III, J. V. *Conscious Millionaire*, 13. Conscious World Press, 2014.

Daskal, Lolly. "7 Reasons the Best Employees Quit, Even When They Like Their Job." 93. https://www.inc.com/lolly-daskal/7-reasons-the-best-employees-quit-even-when-they-like-their-job.html.

"Engaged Employees Infographic." Dale Carnegie Training. 20. https://www.dalecarnegie.com/employee-engagement/ engaged-employees-infographic/.

Hartung, Adam. *Create Marketplace Disruption*, 40. FT Press, 2009.

Lesonsky, Rieva. "It's 2017. How Can You Not Have a Website Yet?" January 3, 2017, 72. https://www.score.org/blog/ its-2017-how-can-you-not-have-website-yet.

Morrison, Kimberly. "81% of Shoppers Conduct Online Research before Buying." November 28, 2014, 72. http://www.adweek. com/digital/81-shoppers-conduct-online-research-making-purchase-infographic/.

Niven, Paul R. *Balanced Scorecard Step by Step*, 62. John Wiley and Sons, 2006.

Patrick, Josh. "Do You Really Expect Your Business to Get You Through Retirement?" *New York Times.com*, September 20, 2010, 35. https://boss.blogs.nytimes.com/2012/09/20/do-you-really-expect-your-business-to-get-you-through-retire-ment/.

Pollack, Scott. "What, Exactly, Is Business Development?" *Forbes. com*, March 21, 2012, 57. https://www.forbes.com/sites/scott-pollack/2012/03/21/what-exactly-is-business-development/ - 2592b1a37fdb.

Shane, Scott. "Learning by Doing and Entrepreneurship." Small Business Trends, 14. https://smallbiztrends.com/2015/06/learning-by-doing-entrepreneurship.html.

Snyder, Benjamin. "Half of Us Quit Our Jobs Because of Bad Bosses." *Fortune*, April 2, 2015, 25. http://fortune.com/2015/04/02/quit-reasons/.

Sorenson, Susan. "How Employee Engagement Drives Growth." *Gallup News*, June 20, 2013, 20. http://news.gallup.com/businessjournal/163130/employee-engagement-drives-growth.aspx.

Tanner, Michael. "Welfare: A Better Deal than Work." August 21, 2013, 83. http://www.nationalreview.com/article/356317/welfare-better-deal-work-michael-tanner.

Thomson, David G. *Blueprint to a Billion*, 57. John Wiley and Sons, 2006.

United States Department of Labor website. January 12, 2018, 24. https://data.bls.gov/timeseries/LNS11300000.

www.ingramcontent.com/pod-product-compliance
Lightning Source LLC
Chambersburg PA
CBHW060616200326
41521CB00007B/784